Foreword

About 30 years ago, my mother was very excited when she obtained a copy of this book. She found it very helpful and knew that it would also help a good friend of hers — called Hugh — who at that time was working in India. I was allowed a brief read of the book then, but it was sent out to India very quickly.

Hugh received and read the book, and expressed appreciation for it, but for some reason it was never returned. It was therefore with great pleasure that I received a copy of this book recently, and have once again enjoyed the writings of Brownlow North — which had brought much spiritual refreshment all these years ago.

As you will discover, this exceptional book brings to life the history of the Israelites as they travelled from Egypt to the Promised Land. I am sure that under God's blessing difficulties in the Christian journey will be resolved as you read the book, and you will wish to share the book with others.

My mothers enthusiasm for this work was "infectious", its message is from above, the author is extremely direct and personal with a word to believer, seeker and the unconverted. You should have no trouble in understanding what he means, you will not be disappointed with what you read:— rather you will be impressed with the truths so lucidly presented.

R W M M
Geanies House
Ross-shire

April 1989

© 1989 Christian Focus Publications Ltd

ISBN 1 871676 04 5

Christian Focus
Publications

Houston · Texas   **Tain · Ross-shire**

OURSELVES
on the journey to freedom

illustrated from
the Book of Exodus

by

Brownlow North, BA
Magdalen Hall, Oxford

CHRISTIAN FOCUS PUBLICATIONS LTD

Contents.

I.

Our Bondage.

THE BONDAGE OF ISRAEL A TYPE.

THE Holy Ghost tells us, in 1 Cor. x. 11, that the things which happened to Israel, "happened unto them for ensamples; and they are written for our admonition, upon whom the ends of the world are come." Persuaded that Israel's history is a type of the history of God's people in all ages, and that the consideration of it is likely to be profitable for doctrine, for reproof, for correction, for instruction in righteousness, I have determined to place before the public this little book, in which I have spoken about some of the things that happened to Israel, as related in that portion of the Holy Scriptures which treats of their bondage in Egypt — their delivery — their wilderness journey—and ultimate arrival in the promised

land.   May God the Holy Spirit bless the
truths that I have written, exceeding abun-
dantly, above all that I can ask or think.

The opening of the Book of Exodus intro-
duces us to the children of Israel lying in the
most cruel bondage.   They were slaves to
Pharaoh and the Egyptians, who "made their
lives bitter, with hard bondage in mortar, and
in brick, and in all manner of service in the
field : all their service, wherein they made
them serve, was with rigour." (Exodus i. 14.)
No people could be more wretched or miserable
—no earthly position could be more abject or
degraded—than the position of the children of
Israel, described in the opening chapters of the
Book of Exodus.

Why has all this been recorded ?   For our
learning.   Their bondage was very bitter—
their slavery was very galling : but, to spiritualize my subject at once, and to bring home
its application to ourselves,—their bondage was
not so terrible as the bondage of every man
and woman born into the world.   Their bondage was temporal,—our's is spiritual ; they
were born the slaves of Pharaoh,—we are born
the slaves of sin ; they were in the power of the
Egyptians,—you and I are by nature in the
power of the devil and his angels.

Dear friends, before I go further, I would beseech you to remember my object in publishing these lectures. It is not to take advantage of my position, and say harsh things; but to try and do good to souls. And if I seem to be uncharitable, or to speak unlovingly, do me the justice to believe I have no desire to be either. I would beg you also not to reject what I say upon your own ideas of truth, but to try my statements by the written Word of God; and before you so try them, pray God, for Christ's sake, to give you His Holy Spirit to open your understanding to understand the Scriptures. Let me entreat you to remember this request.

In what I am about to say my desire is to awaken the attention of lost sinners; and my prayer to God is, that each sinner, into whose hands this book may fall, may be arrested by my words, and aroused to a sense of his position. The wrath of God abideth on him, and he does not feel it: but, if possible, I would make him feel it; for until he does, he will care nothing for the salvation that is provided for him. If there was no hope for him, I would leave him alone, and let him go on undisturbed by me to his miserable ending: but there is hope for him though he is the greatest sinner out of hell,—for the Scripture says, that "to him that is joined to all the living there is hope." (Eccles. ix. 4.) Therefore, so far from leaving him, I would cry to him, as Paul cried to the Ephesians, "Awake, thou that sleepest, and arise from the dead, and Christ shall give thee light."

I say then, again, that no Egyptian bondage was ever nearly so cruel, so degrading, or so hopeless, as the bondage in which you and I were born, the fallen sons of Adam. Satan is the prince of this world; and every child of Adam is born, not into the kingdom of God, but into the kingdom of Satan. He is born his subject, his slave. His reason, his senses, his perceptions are all under his influence: he not only acts, and speaks, but actually thinks, as he would have him: he can neither see, nor hear, nor feel, but as he teaches him. So total is his bondage, and so servile his subjection, that when God says one thing, and the devil another, he believes the devil, and makes God a liar!

Remember, I am not speaking of earthly, but of spiritual bondage; and God's Word bears me out in the statement, that so thorough is man's captivity to Satan by nature, and so absolute his rule over him, that for all the

purposes for which God sent him into the
world, he is *altogether and thoroughly dead*. It
is true, he has natural eyesight, natural hearing, and all the other natural senses; he can
do anything to promote his own interests in
the things of time and sense; he has been
known to gain the whole world by his own
wisdom and power, and then sit down and weep
because there were no more worlds to conquer:
but the natural man has no *spiritual life or light*,
—not one particle.

*No man ever yet followed the guidance of his
natural spirit from his birth to his grave, who did
not dishonour God, and lose his own soul.* All
spiritual wisdom left him when God left him
at the fall; and so the Scripture tells us (1
Cor. ii. 14): "The natural man receiveth not
the things of the Spirit of God; for they are
foolishness unto him:" and again, that "he
cannot know them, because they are spiritually
discerned." He has by nature no Holy Spirit
to teach him. He has the Spirit that is in the
world, and so can discern worldly things; but
he has *no Holy Spirit*, and so cannot discern
spiritual things; and therefore, when I talk to
you, who really are deaf, and blind, and captive,
about your deafness and your blindness, and
about your worse than Egyptian bondage—

though it is a perfectly true picture of what you really are,—yet I seem to you as one that is speaking folly.

Such is the bondage in which Satan holds the natural man, that not only has he no truth in him, but *he has actually no power to receive the truth when it is put before him.* He has no more spiritual power to receive spiritual food than a corpse has to receive natural food. He is dead—not naturally—Adam did not die *naturally* in the day that he sinned,—he lived many hundred years afterwards; but he died SPIRITUALLY, and all his seed in him, so that every natural man is born dead SPIRITUALLY.

Dear friends, these are solemn statements, and surely they should make every unconverted man who hears them, THINK. Do you feel no interest in your heart about your eternal future? If you do not, should not the very fact that you do not, alarm you? Whose do you think is the power that is exercising this tremendous influence over you? Ask yourself!

You profess to believe that you are immortal; that the day of your death will come; that the day of your judgment, and the day of your eternal fixedness in heaven or in hell will come; and yet you are living without the slightest particle of concern or anxiety about the matter! Surely this is something worse than Egyptian bondage. It is nothing more or less than *devilish bondage.* You profess to believe the Bible; you confess that you are immortal; you know that you are to spend that immortality in everlasting misery or everlasting glory; you know that the Bible is against you, and that if you die as you are, it will be misery and not glory; and yet you are uninterested about the matter,—have not as much anxiety about where you are to pass eternity as will lead you to take one step, nay, not even to put up one prayer to God, through Jesus Christ, to deliver you out of your terrible bondage. Oh, what a bondage it is! Bound by the cares, and the pleasures, and the "other things" of this world; so bound that you put them before God, and Christ, and your own immortal soul.

Am I wrong in saying you are a slave?— and a slave to the hardest taskmaster in the whole world,—even the slave of Satan. And is he not at this very moment doing what he pleases with you,—leading you captive at his will, down the broad road to everlasting destruction? And will not everlasting destruction most surely be your portion, if you are not delivered from his power?

What are you to do then?—Despair? God

forbid! The history of the children of Israel
was written expressly for Satan's captives,
that they might not despair, but have hope.
The same God that delivered them, is able and
willing to deliver you, and He says unto you,
"Fear not: believe only." Believe in that
Jesus, whom He Himself has exalted to be a
Prince and a Saviour—to give deliverance to
the captives—recovering of sight to the blind
—and to set at liberty them that are bound.
Believe in that Jesus who says, "Him that
cometh to Me I will in no wise cast out;" and
of whom the Holy Ghost bears record that
"He is able to save to the uttermost them that
come unto God by Him." (Heb. vii. 25.) That
He can and will deliver every sinner that puts
his trust in Him, are the glad tidings of great
joy which this same Saviour commanded should
be preached *to every creature;* and, no matter
who or what you are, if you believe on the
Lord Jesus Christ you shall be saved.

I cannot dwell longer on this part of my
subject: before leaving it, however, I would
pray God the Holy Ghost to teach you to
receive this fundamental truth,—that *you never
can receive any spiritual deliverance until you
acknowledge and feel your spiritual bondage.* The
children of Israel felt it bitterly, for we read

(Exod. ii. 23), that they "sighed by reason of the bondage; and they cried, and their cry came up unto God." And this is why I say you can have no deliverance till you feel your bondage: for until you feel it, *no cry will go up from you to God*, and God has said "*I will be enquired of.*" (Ezek. xxxvi. 37.)

It is a good sign, both OF a man, and FOR a man, when his burdens make themselves felt and he begins to cry to God. *It is a sign of life.* A dead thing cannot cry, but the first thing a child does when it is born is to begin to cry: it is a sign it is a living child; it is a sign also that it feels itself a poor and needy child; and its cry is at once its confession of helplessness and its prayer for help. So with the child of God: the Holy Ghost convinces Him of sin,—of his own sin; opens his eyes to see that he is poor, and blind, and naked, and lost, and miserable; and that unless he is born again of the Spirit, it would be better for him that he had never been born at all: and then he does what these Israelites did,—he cries unto God; and God does to him what He did to these Israelites,—He hears his cry, and comes down to deliver him.

II.

Tidings of Deliverance.

"God come down to Deliver."

You know the history of Moses. Let us look at it first, as given us by St. Paul, in Hebrews xi.

"By faith Moses, when he was born, was hid three months of his parents, because they saw he was a proper child; and they were not afraid of the king's commandment. By faith Moses, when he was come to years, refused to be called the son of Pharaoh's daughter; choosing rather to suffer affliction with the people of God, than to enjoy the pleasures of sin for a season; esteeming the reproach of Christ greater riches than the treasures in Egypt: for he had respect unto the recompense of the reward. By faith he forsook Egypt, not fearing the wrath of the king: for he endured, as seeing Him who is invisible."

Now I will present this man Moses to you, as he is introduced to us in the beginning of Exodus iii., keeping the flock of Jethro, his father-in-law. It is written: "Now Moses kept the flock of Jethro, his father-in-law, the priest of Midian: and he led the flock to the backside of the desert, and came to the mountain of God, even to Horeb. And the Angel of the Lord appeared unto him in a flame of fire out of the midst of a bush: and he looked, and, behold, the bush burned with fire, and the bush was not consumed. And Moses said, I will now turn aside, and see this great sight, why the bush is not burned. And when the Lord saw that he turned aside to see, God called unto him out of the midst of the bush, and said, Moses, Moses. And he said, Here am I. And He said, Draw not nigh hither: put off thy shoes from off thy feet, for the place whereon thou standest is holy ground. And the Lord said, I have surely seen the affliction of my people which are in Egypt, and have heard their cry by reason of their taskmasters; for I know their sorrows; and I am come down to deliver them."

"*I know their sorrows; and I am come down to deliver them.*" Wonderful words from the mouth of the living God! And not for Moses'

sake only, or for the Israelites of that day
were they spoken; but if we are amongst the
number of God's suffering, praying people, for
our sakes also.

"*I know their sorrows.*" God knows the
sorrows of His people. The answer to prayer
may not come as we expect; the burden may
not be removed as immediately as we would
desire; but though our own hearts are over-
whelmed within us, *God knows our sorrows;*
and we may be quite sure, if we only trust
Him, that in His own time, and in the very
best way, though perhaps in a way that we
little looked for, He will give us a happy
deliverance out of them all. "Trust in Him,"
says the Psalmist, "AT ALL TIMES." (Psalm
lxii. 8.) *And when is the time that is not a time?*

Again, not only does the Lord say, "I know
their sorrows;" but, "*I am come down to deliver.*"

GOD COME DOWN TO DELIVER! God, not
only acquainting Himself with the sorrows of
His sinful people, but coming down from
heaven to deliver them! Yet so it was,—so it
has ever been,—and so it must ever be, or no
flesh can be saved. There can be no deliverance from the power of Satan unless God
Himself comes down to effect it.

Was it not so when our first parents sinned,

and Adam heard the voice of the Lord God in the garden, crying, "Adam, where art thou?" Did not God, even then, in this earliest stage of man's fall, come down to seek and to save that which was lost?

Was it not so when Israel, God's people, were to be delivered out of the land of Egypt? "I have seen the affliction of my people, and I am come down to deliver them."

Was it not so when the world was to be redeemed out of the hands of Satan, and poor sinners translated from his bondage into the glorious liberty of the children of God? Did not God then come down to deliver? Was not—oh, marvellous wisdom! and oh, marvellous love!—was not a body prepared HIM, that He might taste death for every man, and redeem His Church with His own blood?

And, lastly, is not the salvation of every individual sinner that ever has been, or ever will be saved, effected by God the Holy Spirit coming down to deliver him,—coming down to make His body the temple of the living God; to open his heart to believe and receive the Scriptures, and to teach him to know God the only true God, and Jesus Christ whom He hath sent? And are we not encouraged to pray to God continually *to come down* and save us?

"Bow the heavens, and come down," is a
Scriptural prayer, written for our learning, and
it has the promise, "God will give His Holy
Spirit to them that ask Him."

But "I am come down to deliver them out of
the hand of the Egyptians," is not the whole
message of mercy from God to Israel; for He
adds (and I beseech you mark it well : for oh,
how much of the believer's peace and strength
depends on his faith in this message of God
to him !)—" and to bring them up out of that
land unto a good land and a large, unto a land
flowing with milk and honey."—I am come
down not merely to deliver them out of the
hands of their enemies, but to lead them and
to guide them through their long wilderness
journey, and never to leave them nor forsake
them, till I place them in full possession of
the land of Canaan.

This is a great promise, and one too little
looked at by many Christians. Christ came
down not merely to deliver us from the punishment of sin ; not merely to die for our sins, that
He might have power on earth to forgive sins ;
but that, having paid our penalty, and cancelled
our debt, He might walk with us, as He did with
these Israelites, through the whole wilderness
journey, *and be with us alway*, even unto the end.

It is not my intention to go regularly through all the striking or typical points in the history of the children of Israel, but to touch merely upon those which I think most likely to be generally instructive; I next, therefore, ask your attention to Exodus iii. 13, 14: namely, Moses' question to God, and God's answer.

"And Moses said unto God, Behold, when I come unto the children of Israel, and shall say unto them, The God of your fathers has sent me unto you; and they shall say to me, What is His name? what shall I say unto them? And God said unto Moses, I AM THAT I AM: and He said, Thus shalt thou say unto the children of Israel, I AM hath sent me unto you."

Now I believe there is nothing more necessary to salvation in the whole Scripture than the reception of this name of God, I AM. So important do I feel it to be, that I think I have alluded to it in every little tract that I have written, and very, very often in my sermons and addresses.* Whenever God has a purpose of mercy, either to an individual or a nation,

* If the reader is acquainted with my Tracts, or has been in the habit of hearing me preach, he may pass on to the next chapter, for he will only find in this what he has in substance heard from me again and again.

His first teaching is, I AM. Surely, then, I cannot do wrong in making it my first teaching. God is about to deliver the children of Israel out of their bondage, and the lesson that He tells the minister by whose hand He will deliver them, to teach them, is, "Say unto the children of Israel, I AM." Do not tell them at present to lay hold of any of my attributes; do not call their attention to my power or my mercy, to my justice or my holiness; but set them, as the first thing they have to do, to grapple with this one great truth, — I AM. The natural eye cannot see Me; the natural ear cannot hear Me; the natural heart cannot receive Me; but for all that, say unto the children of Israel, I AM; *and tell them to believe it.*

That this is *the first truth* a poor sinner has to receive, is the teaching of the New Testament as well as of the Old. Often have I startled congregations, by saying that I would tell them what was the first verse in the whole Bible that they should strive to get engraven on their hearts; that until they had that verse, no matter what else they had, they had practically no religion at all; and then I have mentioned Heb. xi. 6 : "Without faith it is impossible to please God : for he that cometh to God must believe that HE IS." Man by nature has no idea that he requires this teaching : God tells him he does, but he does not believe God. God says, in Psalm xiv., "The fool" (that is, the natural man, the unconverted man—for they are all synonymous terms in Scripture) "the fool hath said in his heart, There is no God;" but the fool has no idea that in his heart he does say so, and that it is practical infidelity that keeps him from being a Christian. Yet do we not all know that God has said if the sinner will turn to Him through Jesus Christ, He will not only forgive him his sins, but He will be his Father, and adopt him (the sinner) for His son; that from that moment all things shall work together for his good; that nothing shall ever again really harm him here; and that when this life is over He will bring him to glory and honour, such as it has not entered into the heart of man to conceive? Look at each of these statements separately, and ask yourself, would any man neglect these things if he believed they were the real offers of a Real Person, able and willing to keep His word? I am persuaded that the man who truly believes that there is such a Person as God; that the God of the Bible, though invisible, is really omnipotent, omnipresent, omniscient; that His eye is ever upon all the sons of men, and His ear, if they will pray, ever open to their prayers,—is not far from the kingdom of heaven.

It was through much tribulation that I myself came to a knowledge that I was one of the fools, who without being the least aware of it, was saying in my heart, There is no God; and of such immense consequence do I believe it to be to expose this little suspected but most fatal form of unbelief, that I will repeat my own experience. May God for Christ's sake bless it.

For many years I lived in utter carelessness about the things of eternity. My object was pleasure—the gratification of the moment; and God was not in all my thoughts; at the same time I was quite sure I believed in God, in Jesus Christ, and the Bible, and was not so bad as the people who said they did not. But when it pleased God, by His Spirit, to make me anxious about my soul; when I was brought to look upon death, and judgment, and heaven, and hell, as great realities, and went to God in real earnest, to seek from Him pardon and His Holy Spirit, in the name and for the sake of Jesus Christ our Lord; I found to my agony, that I had not yet got hold of that first Bible truth,—GOD IS.

I am very anxious to make my reader understand what I wish to convey. You know what it is to be in the same room with a person : you believe that person can see you ; and when you speak to him he can hear you ; that when you ask him anything—if you believe he will speak the truth—you attend to what *he says* and never think about what *you feel*. Now, I could not thus believe in the presence of God in the room with me. I could not feel satisfied that He saw me and heard me, as I feel satisfied that a fellow-creature sees and hears me ; the consequence was I put no real faith in His Word, and so got no peace from it. When I cried, "Forgive me, for Christ Jesus' sake," I had not the realizing certainty that He heard me, as I should have if I spoke to you. I said I believed in God, and I thought I believed in God ; but if I could not believe that the God to whom I prayed could see and hear me, what was my God better then the gods of the heathen, of whom it is recorded, "Eyes have they, but they see not ; they have ears, but they hear not." I could, and did pray ; but I had no realizing faith,—yet the Scripture I have already quoted (Heb. xi. 6), putting this degree of faith at the very lowest and smallest grain, says that "without faith it is impossible to please Him : for he that cometh

to God must believe,"—*not feel, observe !*—but
" BELIEVE THAT HE IS."

Now, have you at this moment more faith
than I had then? Do *you* believe GOD IS?
You may say your prayers; you may go to
church: you may be a decent, moral, respectable, and even what the world calls a religious
person; but unless when you speak to God you
believe that HE IS, you have no true religion
in you.   I believe that some people think
themselves better the day they *say their prayers*,
as they call it, than the day they do not; but
if such a man believed that GOD IS,—if, when
he knelt down to *say his prayers*, he believed
that the Person he called God was present, and
saw his heart,—would he dare to *say the prayers*
he does?   He knows very well, if he thinks at
all, that he is mocking God, and that he does not
want what he prays for.   Take for instance, the
petition in the Lord's prayer, "Thy kingdom
come: " suppose that in answer to the prayer
of many who say these words with their lips, the
heavens were to open, and the Lord was to come,
—what would they do? They would call on the
rocks to hide them, and the hills to cover them.
*Be sure that if you dare to profess to pray to God
for a thing you do not want, you have not yet got
that grain of mustard seed of faith,* "GOD IS."

Did you ever in your whole life try to speak to God, wanting to get something from God, and to get your answer direct from God? Read my question again, and think over it for a moment. If you never did, do not say until you have tried, that you believe GOD IS. You can ascertain it in a moment. You would surely like to have your sins forgiven: pray, then to God to forgive you your sins. Lift up your heart, and say "Oh, God, forgive me for Jesus Christ's sake!" Now, can you absolutely say, as in the presence of God, that you believe that He to whom you have professed to make that prayer, knows that you have made it to Him. I am not now speaking of God's answering prayer, I am speaking of His seeing, of His hearing, of His knowing.—Can you really believe that God who made your ear, and made your eye, can see and hear, and does see and hear, all you think and say and do? If so, bless God for it, for then, at least, you believe that HE IS; if not, you have yet to learn this first lesson, before you can be delivered from your house of bondage.

It is the want of this faith that sends anxious souls so often to seek the answer to their prayers in their own hearts, and not from the Word of that God to whom they profess to

pray. They shut their doors and pray to their
Father, who really is in secret with them, listening to them, and most willing to grant them
every grace that they require ; but through
unbelief they do not see Him who is Invisible,
and so they take their answer from their own
feelings, instead of from what He says.   (Heb.
xi. 27.)

Suppose, for instance, it pleased the Lord
to appear in our midst, as He did in the midst
of the disciples after His resurrection, or as
He did to Thomas ; should we not at once
fall at His feet, and cry to Him, Lord, forgive
us our sins, and save us ?   And suppose each
one, who so prayed, heard His precious voice,
saying to him or to her individually, "I died
for the ungodly, I will in no wise cast you out !
Fear not, only believe : My blood cleanseth
from all sin !   I will give you my Holy Spirit !
I will never leave you, nor forsake you !   As
thy day, so shall thy strength be !"—would
you not be sure that you were forgiven, and
rejoice in the certainty of your salvation ?
Would you look to what *you felt or to what
He said ?*   Would His WORD or your feelings
be the warrant for your faith, and the ground
of your peace, and hope, and joy ?   Yet have
you not every one of these precious words,

and very, very many more, all proceeding out of His mouth, and recorded for every one who will believe in what He says, and rest upon it? And does anything prevent you from the appropriation of these precious words to yourself, when you speak to Him and pray to Him, but the not believing that HE IS, as literally as if you saw Him standing by you?—*Consider what I say.*

Under God's blessing, two things helped me to this faith, so far as I have it,—one a logical fact, the other a scriptural revelation. The first came to me thus: either God never saw me,—knows nothing of my past life of sin,—and consequently can never punish me for it; or, He must be seeing me now that I am coming to Him in the name of Jesus. That He had seen the sin, and would punish me for it, was too fearfully impressed on my mind for me to doubt it for a moment. "I was *convinced* of sin." Then, I argued,—as sure as He has seen my sin, so sure He now sees me on my knees, asking pardon in the name of Jesus. Either He had never seen me, or He must always see me: I knew He had seen me; then it followed that He did see me. The thought gave me peace at once. I took the answer to my prayer from what HE SAID, Who was in my room with me. My burden fell off, *and I rejoiced in a pardon, according to the Word of the Lord.* I was seven months in unbelief, however, and in consequent soul-agony, before I got this.

But I said my faith that HE IS was greatly helped by a scriptural revelation. In Psalm cxlv. 18, it is written: "The Lord is nigh unto all them that call upon Him, to all that call upon Him in truth." It was a long time after I had got what I have called "the logical fact," that I saw the comfort to be derived from this revealed truth, by all who desire, as I did, a personal dealing with a Personal God. As surely as the Bible is true, it follows from this Scripture that when a man goes down upon his knees and truly calls upon God to come and listen to him, that the Lord IS NIGH UNTO THAT MAN, WHETHER HE FEELS IT OR NOT.

To conclude this part of my subject,—Was it not the knowledge of the presence of the great I AM, that was the sustaining power of the Man Christ Jesus. So St. Peter interprets Psalm xvi. 8, in Acts ii. 25: "I foresaw the Lord always before my face, for He is on my right hand, that I should not be moved."

Never for one moment, except in that awful hour when He was wounded for our transgressions, and the agonizing cry was wrung from Him, "My God, my God, why hast Thou forsaken Me?" did our blessed Saviour lose sight of His heavenly Father. No matter what the suffering, the trial, or the temptation, —JESUS SAW THE LORD ALWAYS BEFORE HIM : *therefore* His heart could ALWAYS rejoice ; *therefore* His tongue could ALWAYS be glad, or sing God's praise ; *therefore* could He say, however hungry or thirsty or weary, " I have meat to eat; *therefore* could he reply to every temptation of the Tempter, " Man shall not live by bread alone, but by every word that proceedeth out of the mouth of God ; " and *therefore* could He, even in the very prospect of death, rest on the unfulfilled promise,— " Moreover also my flesh shall rest in hope, because Thou wilt not leave my soul in hell, neither wilt Thou suffer Thine Holy One to see corruption." Such victories as these, over the world, the flesh, and the devil, are ours, in proportion as we see THE LORD ALWAYS BEFORE US, and realize this fundamental truth of God's teaching,—I AM.

I have written thus at length on this subject, because I feel the belief in the Personality and

real though invisible presence of God, to be
essential to the existence of true religion in
the soul; for without this faith it is impossible
to please Him, for "he that cometh to God
must believe that HE IS, and that He is a
Rewarder of them that diligently seek Him."

III

The Demand: its Reception: The Promise.

GOD then in His mercy looked upon the affliction of the children of Israel, and sent Moses to tell them that He had come down to deliver them.

Let me once more, for a moment, call your attention to the state these Israelites were in when this message first reached them. *They were in bondage.* It had probably never entered into the heart of any one of them that they ever could be delivered. Their captivity appeared hopeless; their taskmasters made them serve with rigour, and there seemed no possibility of escape.

And thus it is that the gospel message always finds the poor sinner. It does not come to him when he has half saved himself; but finding him completely under the guidance of that false

teacher, his own heart—tied and bound by his
sins, and led captive by Satan at his will—it
tells him that God has come down to deliver
him ; that Jesus of Nazareth has died to save
him ; and that, having been anointed with the
Holy Ghost, and with power, it is His express
mission to loose the prisoners, give deliverance
to the captives, and save out of the hands of
their enemies, all those that come to God by
Him. The message that Moses delivered to
these Israelites is but the message that every
faithful minister of God has ever since delivered
to his congregation, and is the message that I
desire to deliver in this little book. Think not
of your captivity : look not at the hopelessness
of your position, or the apparent impossibility
of your deliverance ; but look at Jesus, the
author of salvation to all them that obey Him
—THE GREAT I AM come down to deliver.

We read, in Exodus iv. 31, that " *the people
believed ; and when they heard that the Lord had
visited the children of Israel, and that He had
looked upon their affliction, then they bowed their
heads and worshipped.*" This is the attitude of
simple childlike faith, and brings glory to God,
and salvation to the sinner. We are not to
reason, not to argue. I grant you that it is
wonderful,—that it is more than could have

entered into the heart of man to conceive, that
God should have so loved the world as to give
His only begotten Son to die for such as we
are,—that at such a cost He should have purchased to Himself the power not only to deliver
us from the guilt, punishment, and dominion
of our sins—but to dwell in us by His Spirit,
—and teach us, and lead us, and never leave
us, until He has brought us safe into His
everlasting kingdom. Well may we inquire,
Is this what He tells us in His Word? Is this
His message to me as a sinner, and written
in His own blood? But once satisfied that *it
is*,—once convinced that "*thus it is written*,"
and that "*thus saith the Lord*," then who am
I, that I should reply against God? These
Israelites *believed, bowed their heads, and worshipped;* and without reason, or cavil, or question, God calls on us to do the same.

The conflict now begins. The Israelites
believed God, and were willing to make an
effort for their deliverance, trusting for their
success to the promise and power of Him who
had come down to deliver them. They agree that
Moses and Aaron should go in unto Pharaoh,
and demand that he should let them go.

Reader, if you are still in his power, will
not you, trusting in the promises of that same

God, who has also come down to deliver
you, demand this day of that great spiritual
Pharaoh, the devil, that he should let you
go. The demand of Moses was a declaration
of war with Pharaoh, for Pharaoh yielded no
obedience to the God of Israel,—and your demand will be a declaration of war with Satan;
but the same God who fought on the side
of Moses will fight for you; and Satan can
no more hold you than Pharaoh could keep
Israel.

We read, "Moses and Aaron went in and
told Pharaoh, Thus saith the Lord God of
Israel, Let my people go, that they may hold
a feast to Me in the wilderness. And Pharaoh
said, Who is the Lord, that I should obey His
voice to let Israel go? *I know not the Lord,
neither will I let Israel go.*"

Such was the first answer of this proud man,
and he spoke truly when he said, "I know not
the Lord;" neither he, nor any other child of
Adam ever knew the Lord, until He was revealed to him by the Lord. (See Matthew
xi. 27.) The very fact that he would not *obey
the Lord* was a proof that he did not *know the
Lord*. But what an acknowledgment! Do you
know what it is a man confesses when he says
he does not know the Lord? *He confesses that*

he is unsaved: that if he were to die as he is, he would perish for ever !

In the Second Epistle to the Thessalonians chap. i. 7, 8, it is written, "The Lord shall be revealed from heaven, with His mighty angels, in flaming fire, taking vengeance on them *that know not God*, and that obey not the Gospel of our Lord Jesus Christ." This Scripture may have escaped your notice; you thought, perhaps, that Jesus Christ would come to take vengeance only upon the outwardly immoral and profane—upon murderers and adulterers—upon fornicators and Sabbath-breakers—upon swearers, drunkards, and such like; but that is not the teaching of the Word of God. That Word says, that those who *know not God*, no matter what their moral character may be, shall be punished with *everlasting destruction*. And the same Word tells us (John xvii. 3) that this is life eternal,—*to know God, the only true God, and Jesus Christ whom He hath sent.*

And what is the counsel of this God to sinners who do not know Him? "Acquaint thyself now with God, and be at peace." (Job xxii. 21.) All our ignorance, and all our misery arises from not knowing God. It is because men do not know God that they do not want to know Him: I believe there are persons who would look with the greatest fear and horror at the idea of spending an hour in a room alone with God. You cannot disturb Satan more in an unconverted man than by asking him,— "Do you know the Lord?"

From whence do such men get their notions about God? FROM THEIR OWN HEARTS. From that heart that is enmity against God. (Rom. viii. 7.) From that heart out of which comes false witness. (Matt. xv. 19.) From that heart which is deceitful above all things, and desperately wicked (Jer. xvii. 9): and which is by nature filled with a spirit whose object is to lie to us while we are in this world, that in the world to come he may destroy us, soul and body, for ever. This is the teacher who gives to every one of us his natural thoughts about God, in order to keep us from wishing to know Him. But there is not one word, from Genesis to Revelation, that should lead any one of us to be afraid of acquainting himself with God. So far from that, the whole teaching of the Bible amounts to this,—that there is no real peace, or joy, or aught worthy of the name of happiness, but that which arises from knowing God, and Jesus Christ whom He hath sent. I can set to my seal that this witness is true; and so can multitudes; and so shall every one who has faith to make his own heart a liar, and to go to God through Jesus Christ for the teaching of His Holy Spirit.

Let me direct your attention to one thing about God: and may His Spirit bless it to you. You acknowledge that HE IS—that in Him you live and move, and have your being— that He doth what seemeth Him good. *Now think, first, what has been your conduct through life to this God, who made you that you might live* FOR HIS GLORY; *and think, secondly, what must be His nature, and His character, when He is still following you with mercy.* He could have cut you down at any time: you have seen Him cut down your relatives, your friends, your neighbours; but He has spared YOU. Nay, more, He condescends to tell you, in 2 Peter iii. 9, what His reason has been for sparing you: He is "*not willing that any should perish, but that all should come to repentance.*" And in the fifteenth verse of that same chapter, He bids you to count the very fact of His having spared you, as a proof that He is still willing to forgive the past, and to save you, if you will only now turn to Him; for thus it is there written, "*Account that the longsuffering of our Lord is salvation.*"

Pharaoh spoke the truth when he said, "I know not the Lord." Had he known God he never would have acted as he did. It is only those who know not God, who dare to contend with the Almighty. But Pharaoh had to learn to know God, and so have you. If you begin now, you will learn to know Him as a God of love, and mercy, and goodness passing knowledge; a God who will take pleasure in doing you service, and will supply all your need out of the abundance of His riches in glory, by Christ Jesus; but if you neglect to learn to know Him while He sits on His mercy seat; if you wait till He has risen up, and enthroned Himself for judgment—then you will learn to know Him as a consuming fire. *Oh, it will be a fearful thing for the man who makes his first acquaintance with God at the day of judgment.*

But some will say, "How am I to acquaint myself with God?" I answer briefly, By studying Him as He has made Himself known unto you in His Word; especially as He is revealed to you by Jesus Christ, who is "the brightness of His glory, and the express image of His Person." No man knows "the Father save the Son, and he to whomsoever the Son will reveal Him." (Matthew xi. 27.)

The study, however, to acquaint yourself with God can never be successful unless you

first seek the teaching of the Holy Spirit,—
for it is written, "the things of God knoweth
no man, but the Spirit of God;" and it is only
those who receive this Spirit *(promised to all
who ask for Him)*, that are able to know the
things that are freely given to us of God.
(1 Cor. ii. 11, 12.) *All things that are needful
for our life and salvation are freely given to us
already, by God in Christ Jesus; but we cannot
know them without the teaching of the Holy Spirit.*
(See on this subject 1 Cor. chapters i., ii., iii.,
beginning at the 16th verse of 1st chapter.)

This first attempt of the Israelites to get
from under the yoke of Pharaoh seemed to
succeed but badly, indeed it rendered their
position apparently more hopeless. Not only
did the King of Egypt refuse to let the people
go, but we read, in Exodus v. 6, that the same
day he commanded "the taskmasters of the
people and their officers, saying, Ye shall no
more give the people straw to make brick, as
heretofore; let them go and gather straw for
themselves. And the tale of the bricks which
they did make heretofore, ye shall lay upon
them; ye shall not diminish aught thereof,
for they be idle: therefore they cry, saying,
Let us go and sacrifice to our God."

Now that such an order, issued by Pharaoh,

should be a great trial, and that Satan should take advantage of it to discourage and dishearten the people, might be expected; still, after the faith they had so lately professed in God, who could have been prepared for the history recorded?

The end of Exodus v. tells us, the people "met Moses and Aaron as they came forth from the presence of Pharaoh, and said unto them, The Lord look upon you, and judge; because ye have made our savour to be abhorred in the eyes of Pharaoh, and in the eyes of his servants, to put a sword in their hand to slay us. And Moses returned unto the Lord, and said, Lord, wherefore hast Thou so evil entreated this people? why is it that Thou hast sent me? For since I came to Pharaoh to speak in Thy name, he hath done evil to this people: neither has Thou delivered thy people at all."

Oh, what an account, not of the people only, but of Moses also! What language could have been more dishonouring to God! What reply could they have made to Him, if He had cast them off for ever! And in what had this sin its origin? *In unbelief!* These Israelites had already forgot "I AM," and believed more in the visible power of Pharaoh than in the invisible power of God.

Reader, beware! The trial is common to Christians, and these Israelites are "OUR-SELVES: A PICTURE."

But how does God act? Does He cast them off for ever? Instead of casting off, He forgave their unbelief, and instead of reproof sent them another precious promise.

"Then the Lord said unto Moses (Exodus vi. 1), "Now shalt thou see what I will do to Pharaoh." Not to *you*, observe!—but "to *Pharaoh*." "Say unto the children of Israel, I am the Lord, and I *will* bring you out from under the burdens of the Egyptians, and *I will* rid you out of their bondage, and *I will* redeem you with a stretched out arm, and with great judgments. And I *will* take you to Me for a people, and I *will* be to you a God: and *ye shall* know that I am the Lord your God, which bringeth you out from under the burdens of the Egyptians; and I *will* bring you in unto the land, concerning the which I did swear to give it to Abraham, to Isaac, and to Jacob; and I *will* give it to you for an heritage: I am the Lord."

What could be more explicit or encouraging than this promise? It is God alone who can say "I WILL," with the certainty that what He wills shall most suerly come to pass. And when He says "*I will be your God*," and "*you shall be my people*," where is the power in heaven, or earth, or hell, that can hinder it? And He does say so to every one who is willing to *rest upon His Word*. As I have said before, it is not what *we are*, that we are to look at. Our burden, our bondage, our impossibilities are all permitted by God, and will work together for our good ; but we are to look not at these, but *at what God says:* and He says to every sinner under the sun, no matter how loaded with sin ôr tied and bound by Satan,— Only believe my Word, as declared in the Gospel of Jesus Christ, and I *will* deliver you, and *you shall be* one of my people, and I will be your God.

IV.

The Conflict.

IN spite of all that Moses could say or do, Pharaoh made up his mind to rebel against God. He determined to enter into conflict with this unknown God, and not to let the children of Israel go. What happened?

First, God sent Moses to him with a word: that would not do. Then with a sign: Aaron cast down his rod before Pharaoh, and it became a serpent: that would not do. And then came a blow—and then another—and another —and another: until at last—his country devastated, his people wasted, his own first-born son a corpse, and not a house in Egypt in which there was not one dead, he rises up in the night, distracted by the terrors of the Lord, calls for Moses and Aaron, and cries, "Get you forth from among my people, both ye and the children of Israel, and go, serve the Lord as ye have said." The Lord getteth Himself the victory, as He ever must get; but oh, how much better would it have been for Pharaoh if he had obeyed Him at the first, and let the people go, according to the Word of the Lord.

Now one of the many solemn lessons we learn from the history of Pharaoh is this,—If God is determined to bring us out to be His people, *nothing can prevent Him;* and if we will not give ourselves to Him at His Word, He will send a BLOW.

I have often thought, and I believe I am not far wrong, that the reason why we see so many of God's dear children a poor, sickly, and afflicted people, arises from the fact that God has been obliged to *strike them* before they would come out from the world. Long before they came out they knew that God was calling them —but they would not come. He called them in youth : He called them when they had health, and strength, and energies, and activities—and they would not come. Then something occurred that made them think for a little while, and they were almost persuaded—but they did not come. Then came a trouble—and, like Pharaoh, they said they would ; but when God removed His hand, like Pharaoh, they broke their word to God; and then came this trial, and then came that; line upon line, and

precept upon precept,—until, by the grace and
mercy of God, and through affliction sanctified
by the Holy Ghost, at last they came out and
gave themselves to God. But, oh, how much
better would it have been, both for His glory
and their own spiritual welfare, if they had
come to Him when He first called them *by His
Word*.

If you, oh reader, know anything of this experience, I beseech you to weigh well what I
am saying. One of two things will surely
happen to you if you continue to refuse to give
yourself to God: He will either strike you or
LET YOU ALONE. Many, blessed be God, con-
strained by the love of Christ, and by the Word
of the Gospel of His Grace, have come to God
without a blow. But if you will not so come,
better far the blow than that God should *let you
alone*. This is the only hopeless state on earth,
—for the man whom God lets alone, *will let God
alone*. I believe there are multitudes of people
in the world who are "let alone" of God.
They once had some good thoughts and good
desires; but they resisted the Holy Ghost, or
backslided. The Holy Ghost said to them,
"Harden not your hearts." They heard His
words, and they hardened their hearts notwith-
standing, and from that time they have never

had any good thoughts : the world may have prospered with them, they have had little trouble or trial,—*but they have been let alone of God, and in consequence they have quite forgotten Him. Their hearts are hardened.*

I believe that many people have lived to a very old age, and spent what the world calls very happy lives, after they had been "*let alone of God.*" It has never troubled them,—they probably have never known it, or thought about it. As others have fallen around them they have chuckled over their yet strong health and buoyant spirits, and boasted how much heartier and happier they were than many younger : a short time afterwards a newspaper paragraph announces their calm and peaceful death. *They had no trials in their life, they had no bands in their death*,—THEIR FIRST TRIAL WAS HELL FIRE.

Oh, these are most awful thoughts, and perhaps disturb you, lest you should be of the number of those who are let alone of God. If they do, YOU ARE NOT YET LET ALONE: for then you would have neither thought nor fear about the matter. No words of mine could rouse you. Such thoughts and fears are prompted by the Holy Spirit ; and he who has them may be sure, *no matter what his past*

life may have been, that he is not yet left of God.
The devil or the heart never prompts such
thoughts or fears as these : they are *good
thoughts*, and come down from God. *But oh,
be careful of them !* "Seek ye the Lord while
He may be found; call ye upon Him while
He is near." If you are thinking of Him, it is
a proof that He is thinking of you ; and if you
will close with His offer of mercy in Jesus
Christ *now*, He will forgive and accept you
now,—for the Holy Ghost says, "*Now* is the
accepted time : *now* is the day of salvation."
But beware of again letting these good thoughts
go ; if you do, that may be *your last*, and God
may for the future LET YOU ALONE: and be
you certain there is no more awful thing on
this side of hell than to be LET ALONE by God.

This "*letting alone*" is called by Moses, in
his history of the children of Israel, "hardening
the heart." Again and again we read, "*the
Lord hardened the heart of Pharaoh;*" this means
God left him to himself—God let his heart alone.

No man needs to have his heart any harder
than it is by nature, in order to make him
resist the commandments of God. Nothing
can make the natural heart of man harder than
it is. In the day that man fell, God left him,
and Satan entered into him, and made his

heart so hard that no power in heaven or earth has ever been able either to soften or to break it. *God Himself never attempts it.* This is a fact not sufficiently recognised by Christians; but nevertheless, it is a fact—that God never attempts to soften our old hearts, or to make them better. When He has a purpose of mercy towards a man, He gives Him *a new heart.* Thus the promise is (Ezekiel xxxvi. 26), "A new heart will I give you, and a new spirit will I put within you." Every saved man and woman on the earth is " a new creature." (2 Cor. v. 17.) He has experienced the new birth —he has been created anew; he has a new heart and a new nature, which produce new affections, and a new obedience, springing from new motives. "Old things have passed away, and all things have become new." "Unless a man is *born again* he cannot see the kingdom of God."

Now Pharaoh had not been born again, and was a type of every natural man, and only acted as every natural man always has acted, and ever will act. Let God leave any man to the power of his own heart, and he will invariably do what Pharaoh did—that is JUST WHAT HE LIKES—and that, not only in the face of the plagues of Egypt, but in the face of EVERLASTING DAMNATION.

I read of no one who up to his day had more done for him, to teach him to know the Lord, than Pharaoh. If any one on earth should have believed that the God of the Hebrews was the one living and true God, Pharaoh was that man. Under the teaching of Moses, and seeing such wonders and miracles before his eyes, he should have believed for the very work's sake. But no : his was the carnal mind that is enmity against God, and only grew harder and harder under that which should have softened it.

Thus it has ever been. Man hears again and again the threatenings of God against sin : he is put in mind of coming death, and of the judgment-day to follow; he is warned from the Word of God, that except he repent he shall most surely perish ; and that not only the wicked shall be turned into hell, but all the people that forget God. (Psalm ix. 17.) And then he is told of the love and mercy of God ; that though he has destroyed himself, if he will believe God, there is not only hope, but certain salvation for him ; salvation not only from the guilt and punishment of sin, but also from its power; that the promise is, " Sin shall not have *dominion* over you;" for " God so loved the world that He gave His only begotten Son that whosoever believeth in Him should not perish, but have everlasting life."

And what are the consequences that follow this preaching? By the grace and mercy of God some receive the message; some believe, and are saved; but too many reject the counsel of God against themselves, *and are hardened*. The same message that is the savour of life to the one is the savour of death to the other. At this very moment what you are reading is either doing you good, or hardening your heart. It is in the very nature of God's messages to do so. If we believe and receive them, they will draw us to Him who sends them; but if we reject them, we acquire a power to go on rejecting them, and every successive rejection renders it less likely that we shall ever receive them at all.

Yet can any one accuse me of injustice, because the Gospel which I preach hardens him, while it softens and saves another? Surely not: the offer is to the one as much as to the other. Rather let such a man cry mightily to God, and beg Him to give him a new heart.

Pharaoh was "without God in the world," so that Satan led him captive at his will; and

Satan leads every man in the same way, who is without the Spirit of God : but had Pharaoh gone to God, God would not have rejected him ; neither will He reject any man, let his present heart be what it may, who goes to Him for a new one through Jesus Christ. (John xiv. 6.)

We have seen what were the consequences of the first attempt of Moses and the children of Israel to escape from the bondage of the Egyptians. So far from letting the people go, Pharaoh was aroused into active rebellion against God, and the situation of the poor Israelites became apparently more hopeless than ever. But we have seen also what God gave them for their consolation : HIS WORD. HIS WORD *that he* WOULD *bring them out from under their burdens ;* HIS WORD *that He* WOULD *take them to Him to be His people ;* HIS WORD *that He* WOULD *be their God, and that He* WOULD *bring them into the promised land.*

To every man amongst them that believed His Word, He fulfilled His promise ; and He will fulfil the same promise to every man, woman, and child on earth, who is willing to be delivered from the bondage of sin and Satan, and, *trusting in the word of the Lord,* to start for the kingdom of heaven.

God sent His word to Pharaoh, " *Let my people go*," and Pharaoh refused to obey; then God sent again—*not a blow*,—but a sign or proof that the message was from Him. "And Moses and Aaron went in unto Pharaoh, and Aaron cast down his rod before Pharaoh, and before his servants, and it became a serpent." This was great mercy, and should have softened Pharaoh. "God does not afflict willingly nor grieve the children of men." (Lam. iii. 33.) He would rather bring us to Himself by the cords of love, if we will be drawn by them; but *if we will not*, His purposes will, for all that, most surely be accomplished; and we may be certain if we neglect His Word, that sooner or later his judgments will follow.

Pharaoh paid as little attention, however, to the sign as he did to the message; his object indeed was to prove that the gods of Egypt were the true gods, rather than the God of Israel.

" Then Pharaoh also called the wise men, and the sorcerers. Now the magicians of Egypt, they also did in like manner with their enchantments;" and though Aaron's rod swallowed up their rods, yet because his magicians could so far imitate the acts of Moses, Pharaoh refused to believe.

Do not many in the present day act exactly in the same manner? False professors and imitators of God's people, men who have a form of godliness without the power, do, like the magicians of Pharaoh, things which bring the Word of God into disrepute; and immediately the world cries out that there is no such thing as true religion, that all its professors are either hypocrites or self-deceivers. And why is this? For the same reason that Pharaoh refused to believe Moses: *they do not wish to believe the religion of the Bible to be true.* It comes to them in the name of the living God, and under penalty of His curse commands them to do what they do not like, and to leave undone what they do like: and they do not wish to be compelled to believe it, for if they do, they have no excuse for not obeying it. Many, like Pharaoh's magicians, can and do imitate it up to a certain point. These changed their rods into serpents, the water into blood, and brought up frogs on the land; but they could go no further. And so men now can say and do a great deal that looks like true religion: but when they are called upon to take up the cross and follow Jesus; to cast out self, and to produce the fruits of the Spirit; having no real living union with

Him from whom all true power is derived, and without whom we can do nothing, their folly is manifest unto all men, as was the folly of Jannes and Jambres. (See 2 Tim. iii. 1—10.)

Pharaoh not only refused to obey the word of God, and let the people go; but refused also to believe the sign that the message of Moses was the Word of God; and so at length God begins to deal with him in judgment. Aaron is commanded to stretch out his rod over the waters, that they may become blood, and he does so.

This first judgment seems to have had but little effect upon Pharaoh; probably because it did not interfere with his own personal comfort so much as it did with that of the great masses of the people,—for water it appears could be got by digging, and the King would be the first supplied; but God's second judgment, the plague of the frogs, which were *upon him* as well as upon his people, compelled for the moment at least his attention, and forced from him a promise that if the affliction were removed, he would obey the commands of the Lord.

"Aaron stretched out his hand over the waters of Egypt, and the frogs came up and covered the land. Then Pharaoh called for Moses and Aaron, and said, Entreat the Lord that He may take away the frogs from me, and from my people, and I will let the people go, that they may do sacrifice unto the Lord."

So said Pharaoh, and perhaps he meant it at the moment: but little did he know his own heart. No sooner was the affliction gone, than the determination to obey God was gone also. Moses and Aaron did pray to the Lord for him, and the Lord heard their prayer, and removed the plague; but "*when Pharaoh saw that there was a respite, he hardened his heart, and hearkened not unto them.*" (Exod. viii. 15.)

How many are there, the religious experience of whose past life exactly coincides with that of Pharaoh up to this point of his history? Perhaps, reader, you are one. God sent to you by the mouth of pious parents, or godly friends, or ministers, and spoke to you about the concerns of your soul. These urged you, as Moses did Pharaoh, in the name of the Lord, to give up persons, and places, and things, that were separating between you and Him, and to let everything go that kept you from Christ, and hindered your soul's salvation; and you would not: then came A BLOW. In some shape or other God laid His hand heavily upon you; and under a sense of suffering you remembered your sin, and cried unto the Lord, promising that if He would take away your affliction, He should be your God, and you would lead a new life, and be obedient to His commandments. God heard your prayer, and the sickness was removed or the trial was taken away; but you have forgotten the vows that you made when you were in trouble, and have gone back to the old places, and the old people, and the old habits.

I say, oh reader, this may be what you have done. If so, I beseech you to pause and consider your position: what is it to end in? Oh, arise now, and cry mightly for mercy in the name of Jesus, before God strikes you again, or leaves you for ever in Satan's power.

When Pharaoh saw that there was respite, he hardened his heart, and harkened not to Moses and Aaron; and then God sent another judgment on him. "And the Lord said unto Moses, Say unto Aaron, Stretch out thy rod, and smite the dust of the land, that it may become lice throughout all the land of Egypt." And they did so, for Aaron stretched out his hand, with his rod, and smote the dust of the earth, and it became lice in man and in beast.

Then said the magicians unto Pharaoh, when they found that they could no longer imitate with their enchantments the works of

Moses and Aaron,—" *This is the finger of God.*"
" And Pharaoh's heart was hardened, and he
hearkened not unto them." (Ex. viii. 19.)

What a picture! a man, with God's hand so
evidently upon him in judgment, that his very
friends and old companions in sin are con-
strained to cry out, "This is the finger of
God: " and he himself so blinded and so hardened as not to see it or hearken! Surely we can
find nothing like this amongst ourselves. Yes!
many are there upon whom the hand of God is
laid in heavy judgment, and these judgments
the direct consequences of their own sins, who
still persist in their reckless wickedness, while
their companions stand by and shudder. Oh,
friend, is it possible that you can be one of
these! If so, do not despair. Humble yourself
under the mighty hand of God, and He will
yet exalt you. Resist the devil, and he will
flee from you. Draw nigh to God, and He will
draw nigh to you. It is not yet too late. These
judgments would have been mercies to Pharaoh
if they had led him to forsake his sins, and
submit himself to God; and so shall all your
trials and miseries be turned into the greatest
blessings, if instead of going on in wickedness
you will even now go to Jesus Christ.

Pharaoh hardened his heart under this

judgment also: and again God sends another.
"And the Lord said unto Moses, Rise up early
in the morning, and stand before Pharaoh, and
say unto him, Thus saith the Lord, Let my
people go, that they may serve Me: else if
thou wilt not let my people go, behold I will
send swarms of flies upon thee, and upon thy
servants, and upon thy people, and into thy
houses; and the houses of the Egyptians shall
be full of swarms of flies, and also the ground
wheron they are. And I will sever in that
day the land of Goschen, in which my people
dwell, that no swarms of flies shall be there,
to the end thou mayest know that I am the
Lord in the midst of the earth. And I will
put a division between my people and thy
people: to-morrow shall this sign be. And
the Lord did so, and there came a grievous
swarm of flies into the house of Pharaoh, and
into his servants' houses, and into all the land
of Egypt: the land was corrupted by reason of
the swarm of flies."

Now, I believe a man is often brought into
such a state of mind, that *while he is in it* he
dares not go on in opposition to God. Divers
are the causes that may produce it; but where
the Spirit of God has not changed the heart,
the effect of such a state is universally the

same. *Instead of yielding himself entirely to God, the man tries to temporize:* his thought is,—How little can I yield to God, and yet deliver myself from His judgment?—How can I escape hell, and yet keep as much of my own way as possible?

This is never the calculation of a soul truly awakened by the Holy Ghost. It is true indeed that the fear of the Lord is the beginning of wisdom, and that the blessed promise has passed the lips of our precious Saviour, that him that cometh to Him, He will in no wise cast out; so that, no matter what is the motive that brings us to Him, *if we will only go to Him*, He will give us faith, and life, and light, and love, and every other thing we need for our salvation. But let none think they are born again, whose obedience to God springs from no higher motive than a mere slavish fear of punishment. Let not such despair, but as sinners go to Christ, and believing in Him, ask that the love of God may be shed abroad in their hearts by the Holy Ghost; and, doing so, let them not fear, for the promise is theirs, —" YOU SHALL HAVE: " but the religion that springs from nothing but a slavish fear of punishment, is the religion of the natural heart of man when the hand of God is on him,

—and when the cause of fear is gone it will influence him no longer.

Such was the religion of Pharaoh. Blow had followed blow in rapid succession, and the judgments of the Lord were heavy upon him. He was obliged also to confess that when the Lord sent troubles and trials He could put a difference between his people and others, and in the midst of evil so preserve His own that no plague should come nigh their dwelling. He saw that there were no flies in the houses of the children of Israel, or on the land of Goschen, where they dwelt; and he began to think that it would be better to be reconciled to the God of Israel, if it could only be managed without much self-sacrifice. In this state of mind he sends for Moses, and proposes to him a COMPROMISE.

"*And Pharaoh called for Moses and for Aaron, and said, Go ye, sacrifice to your God* IN THE LAND."

V.

The Four Compromises.

THE FIRST.
" Go ye and Sacrifice to your God in the Land."

Now this is the first of four compromises that Pharaoh endeavoured to make with God, in order to avoid obeying, in its simple sense, His commandment, *" Let the people go;"* and I beseech you to give me your prayerful attention while I bring the whole four before you, and endeavour to show how precisely similar they are to the compromising suggestions still injected into us by Satan.

As God called Israel of old to come out of Egypt, so He now calls on His people to come out from the world; and the same struggle is yet going on between the natural man and God's Spirit in the heart of the sinner, as went on between Pharaoh and God in the land of

Egypt. The sinner is awakened, he is afraid of God's judgments, he has become anxious about his soul, he wishes to be a Christian; but then he wishes also to keep the world. What is to be done? Satan whispers to him what he prompted Pharaoh to propose to Moses,—"Sacrifice to your God IN THE LAND."

Now every one of us may receive it as a fundamental truth of God, that such a compromise is simply impossible: *you cannot serve God and mammon.* There are two distinct kingdoms on earth, and only two, and each kingdom has its own ruler. The one is the kingdom of this world, of which Satan is the prince; the other is the kingdom of God's dear Son, of which Jesus Christ is King. The subjects of these two are at utter variance; they have no single thing in common. Their belief, their habits, their customs, their laws, their opinions, their pursuits, their aims are all antagonistic; the objects of the one are temporal, the objects of the other are eternal; and what makes for the welfare of the one is proportionately hurtful to the interests of the other. As well might a man profess to be a good and loyal subject to his Sovereign while openly fighting against him in the ranks of

his enemies, as for a man to call himself a
Christian whose conduct and conversation is
according to the course of this world, and who
makes no endeavour to separate himself from
the impenitent and the ungodly.

I know that I have now come to a part of
my subject which is sure to stir up the enmity
of Satan, for it strikes at the very root of his
power and dominion. He will allow people,
with little hindrance from him, to go great
lengths in religion; they may do many things
that look peculiar and strange in the eyes of
the world, if they will only remain *in the world*
and do them : for so long as they do that, they
are still his subjects : their religion may bring
quiet to their consciences, but well he knows
that it will never save their souls.

But what an opposition does Satan raise in
the heart, when the Spirit of God tells a man
that He will not be satisfied with anything
short of *his coming out from the world;* that
the command to those He receives is, " Come
out from among them, and be ye separate,
and touch not the unclean thing." (2 Cor. vi. 17.)
What struggles he makes to effect a compromise and to avoid the direct conclusion from
this and such-like Scriptures. Oh, how many
consciences there are that bear witness to the

truth of what I am saying! Well do they know that the religion that tells them they can remain in the world, and yet serve God acceptably, is mere self-deception; that God demands their separation, and will be satisfied with nothing less. But though they know it, yet, like Pharaoh they cannot make up their minds to let everything go : they are still, and peradventure have long been, trying to effect a compromise, and the consequence has been they have never yet really come out: they are STILL IN THE LAND.

Oh, let such pause, and consider the import of these words, "STILL IN THE LAND." It is very simple, but very awful. It is STILL IN SATAN'S KINGDOM, STILL IN SATAN'S POWER. Like Herod, you have listened to faithful preachers, and done many things; like Felix, you have trembled ; like Agrippa, you have been almost persuaded to become a Christian ; but you know in your heart of hearts that you have never thoroughly come out from Egypt; that you are still IN THE LAND, and consequently STILL UNSAVED.

But some will say, What is the world? How would you define that from which you tell us we must separate ?

Now, I believe that every man knows quite

well what God means by the world, if he will only be honest, but he asks the question in the same spirit that Pharaoh asked of Moses, "Who are they that shall go?" His hope is that the answer may not be quite so sweeping and uncompromising as his own conscience teaches him it must be.

I would define the world to be A COMPOUND OF PERSONS, AND PLACES, AND PURSUITS WHICH DO NOT GLORIFY GOD, AND WHICH BRING NO HONOUR TO THE NAME OF JESUS.

That man cannot be said to be coming out from the world who habitually associates, on terms of intimacy and friendship, with persons to whom he cannot freely talk about Jesus.

That man cannot be said to be coming out from the world who seeks his amusement in places to which he knows it would be mockery to ask Jesus to go with him.

That man cannot be said to be coming out from the world who, for the sake of any temporal advantage, engages in pursuits on which he cannot kneel down and ask God's blessing.

Or let us take the converse.

He who, under the guidance of the Spirit of God, chooses his companions from those whose conduct and conversation evidence that they love the Lord;

*He who, believing the promise that Jesus is with
His people alway, refuses to mix for his own
pleasure in societies, or go to places where he has
reason to think His Holy Spirit might be grieved ;*

*He who, knowing that it will profit a man
nothing if he gains the whole world and loses his
own soul, seeks, before all the honours and riches of
the earth, the kingdom of God and the righteousness
thereof,* MAY BE SAID TO BE ENDEAVOURING TO
OBEY THE COMMANDMENT, AND TO BE COMING OUT
FROM THE WORLD.

I know that, in opposition to this, it may
with truth be urged that Jesus did not so come
out. When He was on the earth He mixed
with all classes of people ; He accepted invita-
tions from Scribes and Pharisees, publicans and
sinners ; He went everywhere, and to every one
that asked Him. And so He did : and I say
to you, " Go thou and do likewise," only *go in
the Spirit of Jesus,* and the question whether
or not you shall come out from the world will
not be left for you to settle.

Jesus went into the world with but one aim
and one object : namely, *to bring glory to God,
to reflect His image, and to try and do good to
sinners.* Jesus went into the world to testify
of it, that *its deeds were evil*. Never was He
long in any man's house without introducing

spiritual conversation. No matter what the company, He rebuked hypocrisy, showed up sin in its true colours, and spake boldly for His Heavenly Father : IF YOU CAN HONESTLY SAY THAT YOU ARE DETERMINED TO TRY AND DO THE SAME, I do not tell you to separate from the world. On the contrary, LIVE IN IT AS NOT OF IT. Go into the world as much as you will, and as much as you can ; but if you act out your purpose with a single eye, *the world will very soon separate from you.*

It is quite possible to have the name of being more religious than your neighbours, and yet for the sake of other qualifications attractive to the world, to be both received and courted,—but this is possible only so long as you neither say nor do anything that can further the ends of Christianity : once let the manner of you speech and conduct be habitually such as is likely either to awaken worldly people, or to arouse and quicken the slumbering people of God who may have been enticed amongst them, and you will very soon find yourself separated from the world, *for the world will separate from you.* As they cast out Jesus so they will cast out you. A life so like His will be a perpetual condemnation of their's, and they will not tolerate it. You have only to commence it, in order to be hated and avoided; or if approached, to be approached as Jesus was, to entangle you in your talk, that they may have somewhat whereof to accuse you.

A story was told me, some time ago, of a man who was requested by his friend to call upon another who had lately come to reside in his neighbourhood, and who had the character of being something more than a merely nominal Christian. I have reason to believe this story to be quite true. "No," was the reply: "I will not call on that man. I hate him. *I understand he is never ten minutes in the room with anybody before he begins to speak to him about Jesus Christ.*"

Now the man who made this reply was no worse than his neighbours, but only said what is in the heart of every unconverted man. There is nothing that the natural man hates so much as an attempt to speak to him about Jesus Christ. Nothing will make him associate with a man who he thinks likely to do it. The only part of a Christian that such men ever like is *the unrenewed part*,—the part that is *not like Jesus*. Unfortunately there is too much of this part in Christians; but in proportion as you reflect Jesus, so in proportion will they avoid and hate you. And if I see a man who professes to be one of God's people remaining in intimate fellowship and communion with the world, I feel compelled to believe one of these two things,—either that the professor himself is a hypocrite, or self-deceived, and so no Christian at all; or that Jesus Christ did not speak the truth when He said, *"No man can serve two masters."*

VI.

The Four Compromises.

THE SECOND, THE THIRD, THE FOURTH.

PHARAOH's next attempt at compromise was
very like the first, and its object is so
self-evident that I need say little about it.
The hand of the Lord was still heavy upon
him, and he was in fear of further judgments.
He saw that on no terms would it be permitted
that the people should remain IN THE LAND,
and so he proposes to let them go in such a
fashion as shall at once appease and satisfy
God, and yet put no impassable barrier between him and them. "And Pharaoh said, I
will let you go, that ye may sacrifice to the
Lord your God in the wilderness, ONLY YE
SHALL NOT GO VERY FAR AWAY." (Exodus viii.
28.)

Now to what did this amount? *I will consent*

*to your going out of Egypt, since I dare no longer
keep you in it, but stay so close upon my border
that our separation shall be but nominal.* This
was the substance of Pharaoh's proposition,
and it is a proposition to which many have
acceded; they have gone out of the world as
to its usual routine of daily outward folly and
ungodliness, but only so far that upon sufficient inducement, be it either for pleasure or
for profit, they can and do return to it. Moses
rejected such a compromise. He knew that it
would not save the people. Have you accepted
it? If so, DO YOU THINK IT WILL SAVE YOU?

After the removal of the judgment that had
wrung this offer from him, the heart of Pharaoh
seems to have become less and less impressible.
Blow followed blow in rapid succession, yet all
to no purpose. The Lord laid His hand upon
the horses, the asses, the camels, the oxen,
the sheep; and all the cattle in the land of
Egypt died. But still we read, "The heart
of Pharaoh was hardened, and he did not let
the people go."

Then God sent upon him bodily affliction:
a judgment upon his person, and upon the
persons of his people. Moses stood before
him, and took ashes of the furnace, and
sprinkled it up towards heaven, and it became

a boil breaking forth with blains ; and the boil was upon the magicians, so that the magicians could not stand before Moses, and it was also upon all the Egyptians; but still he hearkened not to God.   And then came the fearful judgment of the hail.   " Moses stretched forth his rod towards heaven, and the Lord sent thunder and hail, and the fire ran along upon the ground; so there was hail, and fire mingled with the hail; very grievous.   And the hail smote throughout all the land of Egypt all that was in the field, both man and beast, and the hail smote every herb of the field ; and broke every tree of the field ; only in the land of Goschen, where the children of Israel were, was there no hail."

This fearful judgment did indeed cause Pharaoh to send for Moses and Aaron, and drew from him the confession, "I have sinned," and the prayer, "Entreat the Lord;" yet no sooner did he see that " the rain, and the hail, and the thunders were ceased," than "he sinned yet more, and hardened his heart, he and his servants, neither would he let the children of Israel go." (Exod. ix. 27—34.)

May God the Spirit teach us the lessons to be learned from these awful histories. It is a certain fact, and one that I fear many who may read this book have proved in their own past experience, that *the more a man resists God, the more able he gets to resist Him;* so that the things which could, and peradventure once did awaken him, are now not only powerless, but actually make him harder. Let such an one remember that he is fighting against God, and that in the end God will most surely get Himself the victory. As He had determined that, in spite of all the opposition of Pharaoh, the Israelites should be separated from the Egyptians, so He has determined that every man shall be separated from his sins. Of course I refer here to the pleasures of sin : the *nature* of the last will remain unchanged for ever. If he will let them go now, and seek God's mercy through Jesus Christ, God will forgive his sins, and save him, the sinner, to be to the praise of His kindness through the ages of eternity; but if not, they will be wrenched from him in the day of death ; and THEN what will he think of those things for the sake of which he has lost his soul ? Oh, I beseech you, submit yourself to God, and give up your sins, lest you be hardened !

This last visitation, however, seems to have made for the time at least some impression,— if not upon Pharaoh himself, at all events upon his servants; for we find when another judg-

ment was threatened, and Moses having denounced it, had gone out from the presence of
Pharaoh, the king, at the instigation of his
servants, recalled him, and proposed HIS THIRD
COMPROMISE.

"And Moses and Aaron came in unto Pharaoh, and said unto him, Thus saith the Lord
God of the Hebrews, How long wilt thou refuse to humble thyself before Me? let my
people go, that they may serve Me. Else, if
thou refuse to let my people go, behold, to-
morrow I will bring the locusts into thy coast :
and he turned himself, and went out from Pharaoh.
And Pharaoh's servants said unto him, How
long shall this man be a snare unto us? let
the men go, that they may serve the Lord their
God: knowest thou not that Egypt is destroyed?
And Moses and Aaron were brought again
unto Pharaoh : and he said unto them, Go,
serve the Lord your God: BUT WHO ARE THEY
THAT SHALL GO ?"

Oh, how desperately wicked, and how wil-
fully blind is the natural heart of man! Pharaoh knew well enough what it was that God
required of him, and what he was to let go,
and so do every one of us. The answer of Moses
is the answer for all ages, and all cases : "We
will go with our young, and with our old,

with our sons and with our daughters, with our flocks and with our herds will we go, for we must hold a feast unto the Lord." It is a sweeping and conclusive answer, but nothing less will do. It includes all that we have, and all that we are. It is, in substance, what Jesus said to the multitude : " Whatsoever he be of you that forsaketh not all that he hath, cannot be my disciple" (Luke xiv. 23); and the demand was replied to by Pharaoh, as it is often replied to now, with what I understand to be an oath.

And he said unto them, "*Let the Lord be so with you, as I will let you go, and your little ones; look to it, for evil is before you.*" As if he had said, "If I do,—if I let you go, *and your little ones*, let the Lord be altogether against me, and with you." This seems to me but a lengthened form of the damnation we so often hear men invoke upon themselves in the present day, and which has been common blasphemy from Pharaoh's time to our own. "*Let the Lord be so with you, as I will let you go, and your little ones. Not so: go now ye that are men, and serve the Lord; for that ye did desire.*" (Exod. x. 10, 11.)

What a proposition ! *Go yourselves: go now ye that are men,—go ye and serve the Lord:*

BUT LEAVE YOUR LITTLE ONES, LEAVE YOUR CHILDREN BOND SLAVES IN THE LAND OF EGYPT.

Ye that are parents, how would you have received such a proposal if it had been made to you? With what horror would it have filled you! Could anything be more monstrous? With what indignation would you have rejected it! What, say you: consent to leave my little ones in the land of Egypt, while I myself escape? God forbid! who would dare even to propose it to me?

That some such would have been the genuine and heart-felt expression of every parent's heart I do not for one moment doubt; but how little do we know OURSELVES. Are there not amongst us many, in this so-called Christian land, who are acting out in their conduct this proposition of Pharaoh? Few things, it is true, can be more horrible; yet I am quite sure that few things are more common. I have known professing Christians not only leave their children IN THE LAND during their childhood; not only send them to worldly schools, and have them trained in every worldly custom, habit, and fashion,—but this *for the avowed purpose of fitting them to serve the gods of the Egyptians; or in other words, to mix in that world from which they themselves declare that they have separated.*

I have known professedly Christian fathers not scruple to introduce their sons into the society of the most worldly of the men of this world, when thereby they thought they could advance their temporal well-doing. I have known them accept situations for them, and place them in occupations where every influence around them was ungodly, and where it was hardly possible to believe that their souls could prosper. I have known mothers, after years of apparent separation from the world, go back into it, *for the openly professed reason of introducing into it their daughters.* I have myself remonstrated with such parents, and have been met with the reply, "*It is my duty to my children!*" "What!" say they, "should I leave my girls to go alone into the world?" "Yes," I answer: "*if you have not authority enough to keep them at home.*" Does not the Saviour say, "He that loveth son or daughter more than Me, is not worthy of Me"? If you do not agree with me in this, I believe that you would have accepted a situation for your child in the household of Pharaoh! I believe you would have gone further, and thought it a most desirable alliance *to have given your daughter in marriage to his son, or to have taken his daughter for your son!*

Be honest now with yourself, whoever you are. Would you object to the marriage of your child, if he to whom she was engaged was everything you could desire, EXCEPT A CHRISTIAN? Multitudes know well—multitudes of the training Christian parents, and multitudes of the trained Christian children— that so far from being averse to it, they would *delight in such a marriage.* To such I say, *Shame on your Christianity!* If temporal interests are of more consequence than eternal, if the things of this world are to take precedence of the things of God, if in short the welfare of the soul is to be made subservient to the interests of the body,—then are such Christians led by the Holy Spirit, and taught of God: but if these propositions are false, and Christians are commanded in the Scriptures to teach their children to seek first, or before all things, the kingdom of God and His righteousness, to count all things but loss for the excellency that is in Christ Jesus, not to be unequally yoked together with unbelievers, and that it will profit a man nothing if he gains the whole world and loses his own soul,— then are these parents doing what the Israelites would have done had they agreed to the proposition of Pharaoh,—*sacrificing their chil-*

dren to devils: professing to go out, and sacrifice unto the Lord, while they leave their little ones *in the land.* To such professors, may be addressed those awful words in Isaiah, " *Your ands are full of blood.*" Let such read Isaiah ι. 11—16. Moses did not even reply to the proposition; his countenance doubtless expressed his horror, and so increased the rage of Pharaoh that he had him driven from his presence. (Exod. x. 3—11.)

But it is a hopeless thing for man to contend with God. He who does so will always find, like Pharaoh, that the consequences of his folly will return on his own head. No sooner was Moses gone out from the presence of Pharaoh than the Lord said unto him, " *Stretch out thy hand over the land of Egypt for the locusts.*"

"And Moses stretched forth his rod over the land of Egypt, and when it was morning, the east wind brought the locusts. They covered the face of the whole earth, so that the land was darkened; and they did eat every herb of the land, and all the fruit of the trees which the hail had left. And there remained not any green thing in the trees, or in the herbs of the field, through all the land of Egypt. "Then Pharaoh called for Moses and Aaron in haste ; and he said, I have sinned against the Lord your God, and against you. Now therefore forgive, I pray thee, my sin only this once, and entreat the Lord your God, that He may take away from me this death only." (Exod. x. 12—17.)

The hand of the Lord was once more heavily laid on Pharaoh,—the fear of destruction was once more in vivid reality before his eyes,— and in his terror, he again sends for the man who in the pride of his heart he had so lately driven from his presence, and cries to him, "I have sinned! Forgive my sin, and entreat the Lord for me." But he had done this before, and that again and again, and will the man he had so indignantly treated entreat for him? or will the God he had so often deceived be entreated? For an answer, see Exodus x. 18, 19. "*And he went out from Pharaoh, and intreated the Lord, and the Lord turned a mighty strong west wind, which took away the locusts.*"

I can conceive nothing more beautiful than this, as an illustration of the character of the Christian man, and of the Christian's God!

And now, convinced of His power, and overcome by His mercy, surely Pharaoh will yield obedience to God's commandments, and send away the people. Alas, no : the natural heart *cannot* be softened! Pharaoh's cries for mercy from first to last had proceeded from nothing but a mere slavish fear of punishment; the Holy Spirit of God had wrought no change in his nature; there was in it neither love nor gratitude, nor the spirit of obedience; and so, though God listened to him, and removed the locusts, he still refused to listen to God, and let the children of Israel go. But, brethren, remember that a man may act this way once too often. Beware, therefore, and never make a promise to God without earnest prayer that the Holy Ghost will enable you to keep it; and making this prayer, depend not upon your own resolutions, but upon *His Spirit, given for Jesus Christ's sake.*

I believe that amongst all those who are now in hell, but who in the days of their flesh were hearers of the Gospel, there is hardly to be found one who in his life time did not purpose and promise to obey God.

And now God sends another judgment; but Pharaoh's heart is hardened, and he still attempts compromise.

"The Lord said unto Moses, Stretch out thine hand toward heaven, that there may be darkness over the land of Egypt, even darkness which may be felt. And Moses stretched forth

his hand toward heaven; and there was a thick
darkness in all the land of Egypt three days:
they saw not one another, neither rose any
from his place for three days: but all the
Children of Israel had light in their dwellings.
And Pharaoh called unto Moses, and said, Go
ye, serve the Lord, only let your flocks and
your herds be stayed: let your little ones also
go with you. And Moses said, Thou must give
us also sacrifices and burnt offerings, that we
may sacrifice unto the Lord our God. Our
cattle also shall go with us; *there shall not a
hoof be left behind;* for thereof must we take
to serve the Lord our God; and we know not
with what we must serve the Lord, until we
come thither."

Now I am quite aware that I have already
said much in this little book that may be
called tautology, but it was impossible to avoid
it. Pharaoh's dealings with God were tautology,—a repetition of rebellion and falsehood;
and God's dealings with Pharaoh were tautology,—a repetition of commandment, of judgment, and of mercy. I will not, however,
dwell long on this fourth and last attempt at
compromise. First, it was, " *Sacrifice to your
God in the land.*" Then, when that would not
do, it was, " *Go, but do not go very far away.*"

Then, "*Go, but let your children stay.*" And now, when the blackness of darkness is before the eyes of Pharaoh, it is, *Go! Go where you will; let your little ones also go with you:* BUT LEAVE YOUR CATTLE IN THE LAND."

Oh, what a wonderful thing is the heart of man! This last cry of Pharaoh's was as if he had said, "Oh, God, do not have Thy way in everything; do not take all away: in some small matter, at least, give way to my natural inclinations, and allow me to keep some minor thing, even though Thou hast ordered me to let it go. *I am willing to obey in all that can be called essential;* but oh, let me keep the cattle: it is such a trifle, and I am giving up so much for Thee!"

Surely, I need not stay to spiritualize this. These compromises, from first to last, were but the desperate strugglings of a soul unwilling to yield all to God, and we must reject them or perish. Moses' reply I have already quoted, and it was instantaneous and decisive: "Our cattle shall go with us; *there shall not an hoof be left behind;* for thereof must we take to serve the Lord our God, and we know not with what we must serve the Lord, until we come thither." We will go out from the land, taking with us everything we have: not our

wives only and our children, so far as we have
power to control them; but our cattle, and our
substance, and all we can call our own; for
we are going into a land of which as yet we
have no knowledge, and we cannot tell until
we come there, what God may call on us to
sacrifice.

Is it possible that, with only this small
difference between them, Pharaoh will once
again enter into conflict with the Almighty:
surely now he will make peace with God, and
let the people go! Who would not have
thought so? But no. Though he had made
up his mind to part with all else besides; yet,
for the sake of these paltry cattle, his opposition became more furious than ever, and he
ordered Moses from his presence, with the
threat, "See my face no more, for in that day
thou seest my face thou shalt die." (Ex. x. 28.)

Alas! for how slight a matter will a man
turn back after being almost persuaded to
become a Christian? May not even you, oh
reader, be saying, If it was not for *this thing
or that*, I would at once close with God's offer
of mercy in Christ Jesus, come out from the
world with all that I have, and start on the
wilderness journey for the heavenly Canaan.
Oh, pause a moment before—*for this thing or*

that—you again reject God's offered mercy; you are making your heart harder every time you do so, and your prospect of salvation less and less likely. It is true you cannot leave "*a hoof behind.*" You must come out with all you have, and all you are. You cannot keep any sin, however small or trivial you may call it, and be Christ's disciple. But what will that thing look like to you in the day of judgment, that you now refuse to part with in order to close with Him? Jesus Himself says—*Count the cost.* Count the cost at which you now escape the cross, and keep the sin; and may God dispose you, as He did Moses, to esteem the reproach of Christ greater riches than all the treasures of Egypt, and to chose rather to suffer affliction with the people of God than to enjoy the pleasures of sin for a season.

And now God is about to send His last judgment on the Egyptians. "And the Lord said unto Moses, Yet will I bring one more plague upon Pharaoh and upon Egypt, afterwards he will let you go. About midnight will I go out into the midst of Egypt, and all the first-born in the land of Egypt shall die; from the first-born of Pharaoh, that sitteth upon his throne, even unto the first-born of the maid-servant that is behind the mill, and all the

first-born of beasts, and there shall be a great
cry throughout all the land of Egypt."

Solemn sentence, and certain of accomplish-
ment, for the mouth of the Lord had spoken
it! But He also speaks of the safety of His
people: "Against the children of Israel shall
not a dog move his tongue" (Exod. xi. 4, 8);
and salvation must be secured for the one,
before judgment can be executed on the other:
*the Egyptians must be spared until every Israelite
is in safety.*

Oh, ungodly world! wilt thou not learn from
these histories? How little dost thou consider
thy obligations to the Lord's people. Remember Lot. Was he not the salvation of Sodom
so long as he was in it; and if there had been
ten righteous in the city, would not God have
spared it for the sake of the ten? Has not the
same God that denounced the doom of the first-
born in Egypt, and executed it so fearfully,
denounced also thy doom? Has He not told
thee that the heavens and the earth that now
are, are kept in store, reserved unto fire, against
the day of judgment and perdition of ungodly
men? It is true that day after day, and month
after month, and year after year have passed
away; and because sentence against their evil
work has not been executed speedily, scoffers

have arisen, who say, "Where is the promise of His coming?" But why is His coming delayed? Why art thou, oh, ungodly world, allowed to go on still in thy ungodliness? Know that it is only for the sake of God's people who are yet amongst thy people. Thou art spared, and wilt be spared until the very last of these has been brought under the shelter of THE BLOOD OF JESUS; but then "*the day of the Lord will come,*" bringing sudden destruction,—even the destruction of eternal death on thee, and all in thee *who know not God, and obey not the Gospel of Jesus Christ.*

Oh, ungodly world! wilt thou not avail thyself of the present respite? God is long-suffering; not willing that any should perish, but that all should come to repentance. Thy sentence has been pronounced, but it has not yet been executed; and a way of escape is open to all in thee who will fly for refuge to the hope set before them in the Gospel.

VII.

The Beginning of Days.

BEFORE then God brings His last judgment on the Egyptians, He makes known to Moses how it may be escaped; or, in other words,—HIS WAY OF SALVATION; and tells him to go and declare it to the people.

"And the Lord spake unto Moses and Aaron in the land of Egypt, saying, This month shall be unto you the beginning of months: it shall be the first month of the year to you.

"Speak ye unto all the congregation of Israel, saying, In the tenth day of this month they shall take to them every man a lamb, according to the house of their fathers, a lamb for an house: and if the household be too little for the lamb, let him and his neighbour next unto his house take it according to the number of the souls: every man according to his eating shall make your count for the lamb.

"Your lamb shall be without blemish, a male

of the first year : ye shall take it out from the sheep or from the goats : and ye shall keep it up until the fourteenth day of the same month ; and the whole assembly of the congregation of Israel shall kill it in the evening.

"And they shall take of the blood, and strike it on the two side posts and on the upper door-post of the houses, wherein they shall eat it.

"And they shall eat the flesh on that night, roast with fire, and unleavened bread; and with bitter herbs they shall eat it. Eat not of it raw, nor sodden at all with water, but roast with fire; his head with his legs, and with the purtenance thereof. And ye shall let nothing of it remain until the morning; and that which remaineth of it until the morning ye shall burn with fire. And thus shall ye eat it ; with your loins girded, your shoes on your feet, and you staff in your hand ; and ye shall eat it in haste : it is the Lord's passover.

"For I will pass through the land of Egypt this night, and will smite all the first-born in the land of Egypt, both man and beast; and against all the gods of Egypt I will execute judgment : I am the Lord. And the blood shall be to you for a token upon the houses where ye are: and when I see the blood I will pass over you and the plague shall not be upon you to destroy you, when I smite the land of Egypt.

"And this day shall be unto you for a memorial; and ye shall keep it a feast to the Lord throughout your generations; ye shall keep it a feast by an ordinance for ever."

Thus saith the Lord,—"*This month shall be unto you the beginning of months, and this day shall be unto you for a memorial.*" What day? What month? Let me make an observation to you on this word of the Lord, before I endeavour to place before you His way of Salvation.

This was the month, and this was the day of the month on which God was about to deliver these Israelites out of the hands of Pharaoh and his people—and it was to be to them *the beginning of days and the beginning of months.* The past was to be reckoned by them as nothing. Henceforth they were to date their life not from the day of their natural birth, but from the day that the Lord delivered them, under the cover of the blood, from the destroying angel, and brought them out of the land of Egypt and out of the house of bondage.

Now, what are we taught by this? Most clearly this truth of God,—*that while we re-*

*main of the world, and in the world, we are in
God's sight* DEAD. It is not until we come out
from the world, and, led by God's Spirit, enter
through Jesus Christ into His kingdom, that
God considers us to be born at all. Until this
new birth takes place, all our works, however
apparently excellent in themselves, are *dead
works*, unprofitable to us, dishonouring to God,
and *partake of the nature of sin.* Such is the
teaching of the Bible,—such is the teaching of
the Articles of the Church of England,—and
such is the teaching of holy men of all de-
nominations, and has been in all ages. If this
then be the truth, and most surely it is the
truth, how more than mad is that man who
after he has once heard of Christ, allows any
portion of his natural life to pass before he
seeks to be born of God, and to get through
Jesus an entrance into the kingdom of heaven.

Remember I am not speaking now of an
entrance into the visible Church of Christ by
baptism, but of that new and spiritual life
which none but God can give, and which our
Lord calls being "born again." A man may
have been made the son of God, *so far as
baptism can make him,* and perish, as did the
rich man in hell, whom Abraham addressed as
"SON." His sonship so far from saving him,

but increased his condemnation; but that man who is once renewed by the Holy Spirit,—once born "not of blood, nor of the will of the flesh, nor of the will of man, but of God," *hath everlasting life*, and is safe for ever; for Jesus has said of such, "THEY SHALL NEVER PERISH, NEITHER SHALL ANY PLUCK THEM OUT OF MY HAND." (John x. 28, 29.)

Now it is this beginning of EVERLASTING DAYS, and an entrance into this EVERLASTING KINGDOM, that I would urge you to seek more, and before all that the world can offer. We are all immortal beings: there was a moment when we came into existence, but there never will come a moment when we shall go out of existence. We have all before us *a life of eternal life*,—or, if I may so call it, *a life of eternal death:* so long as God is, we shall be, be it in heaven or in hell: and the sixty or seventy years of our sojourn on this earth is all that is allotted to us out of this never-ending, everlasting existence, to prepare our portion for that kingdom in which we are to spend eternity. Oh, it is awful to see how diligent some men are in preparing *a rich portion for hell;* but it is also solemn and most instructive to consider how much men lose by not preparing *a rich portion for heaven.*

Look at the man who has come to middle life before he has begun to seek the everlasting kingdom of God : should he ever seek it and be saved, if there could be regret in heaven he is the man who would feel it. I speak with some experience on this subject. I was myself more than forty years of age before I went to God in earnest about my soul : and what was then the prayer I was obliged to make to God ? —" *Oh God, for Jesus' sake, forget the past forty years of my life,—blot them in mercy out of the book of Thy remembrance.*" I believe (Lord help mine unbelief) that prayer was heard and answered ; and that God for Christ's sake remembers those forty years no more. But oh, who can calculate the eternal loss that has been suffered ? If, instead of spending those forty years according to the counsels of my own heart, I had spent them according to the teaching of the Holy Spirit, what glory might I not have brought to Christ, and what *durable* benefit to my own soul. But I did not so spend them, and they were lost ; and I was lost also,—till Christ in His mercy came to seek and to save me, and by saying " LIVE," to a man who had been dead for more than forty years, proved that nothing was too hard for Him. That month was to me the beginning of months, and I pray God that that day may ever be to me for a memorial.

Surely such thoughts as these are calculated to make time appear very valuable. Not a moment of our life ever comes to us in which, if we employ it as the Holy Ghost would have us, we may not bring glory to God, and lay up treasure for ourselves in heaven; and every moment that is not so employed is A MOMENT LOST. Not only in active service, but whether we eat, or whether we drink, we may bring glory to God, and when we glorify Him, we benefit ourselves. The counsel of Christ to His saved people is, "Lay up treasure in heaven;" and He does not scruple to call that man A FOOL who heapeth up earthly riches for himself, and is not RICH,—not saved only, but RICH towards God. "Thou fool," is His address to the man who boasted that he had much goods laid up for many years,—"Thou fool, this night thy soul shall be required of thee, then whose shall those things be which thou hast provided?" and then he adds this little recognized, but most solemn truth, "So is he *(a fool)* that layeth up treasure for himself, and is not RICH towards God."

Should we not then inquire diligently, each one for himself, whether we are amongst these

fools in God's sight? Are there not many
who, if they have not already lost forty, have
lost a dozen, sixteen, eighteen, or twenty years
of this time of exceeding value; and who, so
far from having laid up treasure in heaven,
have never even entered into God's kingdom?

Oh, let me ask such, Does not the recollec-
tion of what you are, when compared with what
you might have been, distress and sadden you?
What have you gained by following the counsels
of your own heart, and refusing to believe on
the Lord Jesus? Can you honestly say, as in
God's presence, that you think you are happier
at this moment in the possession of what you
have got through following your own will than
you would have been if you had followed His?
Has the past paid you? Will the future pay
you if you still listen to the same counsellor?
You heard of Jesus when you were a child,
and He asked you to take His yoke upon you,
and to learn of Him, and YOU WOULD NOT; and
you are now twenty, or thirty, perhaps sixty or
seventy years of age, and if you were to die
this moment, so far from having treasure in
heaven, *your portion would* BE HELL, *without even
a drop of water to cool your tongue.*

Oh, if you had taken up your cross and
followed Christ when He first called you,—if

instead of the life-time on which you have to look back, you could look back on a life-time spent in His service, and of treasure laid up in heaven, how rich and how truly happy you would be. And even if you should be spared for years to come, and still go on under the leading and teaching of *your own spirit*, do you think the future will be more profitable than the past? Be not deceived! Listen no longer to the voice of your own lying heart. You have already lost what worlds could not re-purchase. Oh, do at once, this very moment, the best thing that is left you to do : ask God for Christ's sake to forgive and forget all the past years of your life, and to help you for the future to believe and follow Jesus, and to lay up treasure in heaven.

Then this shall be to you indeed a spiritual birthday,—the beginning of months, and the beginning of days; and peradventure the Lord, who is very good, and with whom nothing is impossible, will yet restore both to you and to me the years which the locusts and the canker-worm have eaten. (Joel ii. 25.)

VIII.

God's Way of Salvation.

"Not by works of righteousness which we have done."

I AM now about to try to place before you a clear and simple statement of God's way of salvation; and for Jesus Christ's sake may the Holy Spirit teach me every word I write, and enable you, oh reader, to receive the truth He teaches.

Now in order to tell you how you can be saved, I shall begin by telling you how you most surely cannot.

I commence with this plain and simple statement,— *You cannot in any way save yourself, either in whole or in part, by your own works.*

YOU CAN, AND HAVE DESTROYED YOURSELF, BUT YOU CANNOT SAVE YOURSELF.

As well might these poor helpless Israelites have attempted to save themselves out of the hands of Pharaoh, *as a sinful child of Adam seek to save himself by his own works.*

I am exceedingly anxious to be very clear and explicit about the impossibility of *salvation by works*, for from what I have both seen and heard, I believe there are multitudes in error, and ill-instructed in this doctrine : twice within a few days, when I was last in London, was the subject brought personally under my notice; once with the request that I would mention it in my public discourses. It may be profitable to tell the circumstances.

The first instance was that of a gentleman, who having heard me preach, told me I had made a statement he had never heard before : —that a man *must be saved* before he could do anything acceptable to God. "Of course I always trusted to my Saviour," he said, "but still I thought it was at the end of life,—after we had done a great many good works, and denied ourselves very much, and lived closely to God for a long time, so as to show Him we were in earnest, that we might hope, through the mercy of God to be saved ; but I never heard until you said it, that a man was to work for God, *not to be saved*, BUT *because he was saved.*"

The other case was at a friend's house, where I was dining before going to preach.

A lady, who I know gives much of her time to God's work, as a teacher in schools, a visitor in charitable establishments and amongst the poor and needy, and who has much opportunity of seeing the different phases and forms of irreligion and self-deceit, in the hearts of a very large class, suddenly turned to me and said,— "I wish you would say something in your address to-night, or write a tract to teach people they cannot be saved by their own works. The doctrine that people can be so saved is running through the length and breadth of London,—*especially amongst the honest and hard-working poor, and the morally upright but bodily deformed and afflicted.*

Now how any man who knows anything of the requirements of God's law, and of the awful shortcomings in his own life and heart, can hold such an opinion, I know not; but these two things occurring both in the same week, and just as I was about to bring the subject in the form of a lecture before the public, determined me, before I try to tell you how you can be saved, to show you (God helping me) how you cannot.

You cannot then be saved, or in any way help your salvation by your own works. Salvation is not a work, *it is a gift*,—the free gift of God to every one without exception who will accept it; and before a man can in any sort or way do anything acceptable to God, he must *accept* this salvation; and when he accepts it, HE IS SAVED.

Every man comes into the world under the same law under which Adam came into it. God said to Adam, "Keep my law and live; but in the day that thou sinnest thou shalt surely die." Adam sinned. He did not commit twenty sins, or fifty, or a hundred sins before he died; he committed one,—and in that day, and for that one sin, he died. God left him; the Spirit of God departed from him, and he became spiritually dead.

Now every one of us has sinned: and if we have sinned—supposing we have only sinned once: and supposing that one sin to be what we consider the very least of sins—still if we appear before God in the day of judgment, with that one little sin upon us, though we have committed no other sin than that, for that one little sin's sake we shall be cast into hell. Do you say this is a hard saying? It may sound so; but it is the truth of God; and I repeat again, with God's Word for my warrant, that if you never committed but one sin in your life, and that one sin the smallest and most excusable that can be imagined, if you appeared with it on you at the day of judgment, THAT ONE SIN WOULD CONDEMN YOU.

Bear with me a little, and I think I shall be able to show you how of necessity this must be so. The day of judgment, remember, is not a day of mercy: THIS is the day of mercy,—THAT is the day of justice. The whole teaching of Satan may be comprehended in two great lies: one, that a man cannot get salvation now, to-day, immediately,—that *that* is impossible; the other, that in some way he will get it at a future time,—if not before, at least at the day of judgment. Dear reader, both of these doctrines are doctrines of the devil, and directly contrary to the teaching of God. God's Word declares that *now* is the accepted time; that *now* is the day of salvation; that this very instant, where you sit or where you stand, He is willing to forgive you, and to receive you; He even BESEECHES YOU to be reconciled *now* (2 Cor. v. 20); BUT THERE IS NO MERCY AT THE DAY OF JUDGMENT. Simply " *Guilty or not guilty?*" "Sinless or not sinless?" will be the question then. Appear at the day of judgment with but one spot, even the smallest spot upon your garments, and YOU ARE LOST FOR EVER.

Let me try and make this clear. Imagine this to be that awful day : you are there,—you stand among the throng of those who are clothed in the spotless robes ; your robe looks clean and spotless also. No creature that has come up with you to the bar of judgment can see a stain upon it ; all looks pure and white, and you are about to enter with the sinless ones into heaven ; when suddenly the all-seeing eye of the Righteous Judge looks upon THE LITTLE SPOT. You are called back,—you are questioned : " What is that spot? What is that little spot on your otherwise spotless robe ? " The answer is left with yourself ; you have yourself to say before the assembled multitudes of heaven, earth, and hell. what is that little spot. And what must you say ? IT IS SIN ! *Sin, oh Lord ! it is sin :* but then it is such a little spot ; such a very, very little one, and done so long ago that I had myself forgotten it.

Answer yourself if you think that pleas like these can save you. You yourself say "*It is sin.*" Can sin go into the kingdom of heaven ? Shall heaven be defiled to let you in ? You dare not say that *that* is possible. Then what

is to become of this little spot? Oh, your agony
as you look at it! How different does it appear
now in the light of God's countenance from
what it did when you looked at it under Satan's
teaching. There it is; that little spot: and
must you be damned for that? Why, the
publicans and the harlots, the murderers and
adulterers, the thieves and drunkards are only
damned; and must you, who were so decent,
and so moral, and so respectable, be condemned
to the same doom with them, for that little sin?
It is clear you must, *unless you can wash it out
or take sin with you into heaven.*

Sin cannot go into heaven, and you cannot
now wash it out. There was a time when
there was a fountain open to you for sin and
uncleanness and many of the publicans and
vilest washed in it and were made clean; but
you thanked God you were not as other men,
and neglected this great salvation; and now
your sin is on you, and, little as you call it,
dooms you to everlasting destruction.

LITTLE SIN! Little, yet so great that nothing
can wash it out but the blood of Jesus! Little,
yet so great that God must be manifested in
the flesh to be wounded for that little transgression, to be brusied for that little iniquity,
before the Lord, the Righteous Judge can blot

it out of the book of His remembrance, and permit the sinner to enter heaven!

Oh, look at the Cross of Christ, and you will never call sin little! Blood was shed there which can cleanse from all sin; the chief of sinners may wash away his sins in it, and be saved; but the most blameless on earth if not washed in it will perish for ever. Thus saith the Lord, " *Whosoever shall offend in one point he is guilty of all*" (James ii. 10); and as well might a criminal think because his offences were not so numerous as those of some others who were to be tried with him, he should escape altogether unpunished in a court of justice, as a sinner think he shall be counted guiltless at the bar of God's judgment-seat, because he had only committed what he calls little sins.

" Who then can be saved?" By his own works, NO ONE: for it is written, " *By the deeds of the law there shall no flesh be justified in His sight*" (Rom. iii. 20); and as if to set this question at rest for ever, it is revealed to us in the 14th Psalm, that " *the Lord looked down from heaven upon the children of men, to see if there were any that did understand and seek God;*" and after the scrutiny this was His testimony— " *They are all gone aside, they are all together become filthy, there is none that doeth good, no not one.*"

Triumphant fiends exulted; angels wondered, and peradventure pitied : but *neither angels nor devils ever imagined that God could be a just God, and yet save poor sinners.* "The wages of sin is death,"—and all had sinned : the demand of God is a sinless, spotless righteousness, and all had come short. His justice and His truth were against man : who then could escape destruction ? Every created intelligency must have answered, "No ONE."

But is anything too hard for God ? His justice and His truth were against us, but on which side was HIS LOVE ? That ever was on the side of His sinful and self-destroyed people. Though we had rebelled against Him, He was not willing that any should perish ; and by His wisdom a plan was devised, and by His love a plan has been accomplished, by which mercy and truth have met together—by which righteousness and peace have embraced each other.

God so loved the world that He spared not His only begotten Son, but freely gave Him up for us all ; and now, instead of its being a faithful saying, that there is no hope for us, because we are all sinners, it "is a faithful saying, and worthy of all acceptation, that *Christ Jesus came into the world to save sinners,*" *even the chief.* (1 Tim i. 15.)

IX.

God's Way of Salvation.

The Life of Christ.

I HAVE just said that the wages of sin is death,—and that the demand of God is a sinless, spotless righteousness. Now, as all have come short of the righteousness, so all have earned the wages of sin; or, as the Apostle says, "*Death passed upon all men, for that all have·sinned.*" (Romans v. 12.) But, thanks be to God for His unspeakable gift of Christ, Jesus has supplied all our need: He came to live for us; He came to die for us. He came to live for us that He might fulfil all righteousness in our stead, that He might magnify the law and make it honourable, and by a life of sinless obedience, bring in an everlasting righteousness; which as St. Paul, in Romans iii. 22, tells us, "is *unto all and upon* *all them that believe.*" He came to die for us also, that when as guilty sinners we went to God for pardon and the Holy Spirit, we might be able to plead with Him what a little child now in glory did plead : "JESUS WAS PUNISHED INSTEAD OF ME." *

Ever remember *that the Life of Christ was as necessary for our salvation as the Death of Christ, — and that both are the gift of God to sinners.*

How clearly was this truth typified by the keeping up of the Pascal Lamb from the tenth day till the fourteenth. "And the Lord spake unto Moses and Aaron in the land of Egypt, saying, *In the tenth day of this month, they shall take to them every man a lamb :—your lamb shall be without blemish, a male of the first year,—and ye shall keep it up till the fourteenth day of the same month.*" Why must it be taken up on the tenth, if it was not to be slain until the fourteenth ? Why might not the lamb have been taken at once from the flock, and brought to the sacrifice ? It was without blemish,—nothing could make it more pure or spotless. But no, that would not have done : it must be kept up from the tenth to the fourteenth—three clear

* See the life of "Ada," written by her Mother.— Nisbet and Co.

days; AFTER THAT its blood was to be shed for
the salvation of God's people Israel. Now,
was not the Holy Ghost thus signifying the
three years of that life of Christ,—a year for
a day, in which *He lived for His people* before
He died for them? It would not have done
had the Paschal lamb been brought from the
fold direct to the house, and slain,—neither
would the work of Christ for us have been
complete if He had only come down from
heaven, shed His blood for us, and gone back.
He Himself tell us that He came to do more
than this,—"I came," says He (Matt. v. 17),
"to fulfil the law:" and had He only died for
us, never would a perfect obedience have been
rendered to the law of God by man; *never by
the obedience of One would many have been made
righteous.* (Rom v. 19.)

I am sure it is most essential that our views
upon this subject should be clear and scriptural,
for many false doctrines concerning it are gone
abroad into the world. It is most plainly taught
by the Word of God that the righteousness in
which a man can stand before God in the day
of judgment, and be passed as guiltless into
heaven, is not a righteousness wrought out by
himself upon earth, and composed of his own
works,—but a righteousness which is THE GIFT

OF GOD. (Rom. v. 17.) It matters not what
else a man may have or a man may be : *if he
has not this righteousness he cannot be saved.*

Upon this point the four first verses of the
tenth of Romans are conclusive. There we
find St. Paul thus praying for and speaking of
his unsaved brethren after the flesh : "My
heart's desire and prayer to God for Israel is,
that they might be saved. For I bear them
record that they have a zeal of God, but *not
according to knowledge.*"

Now observe : here are a people very anxious
to please God. Speaking by the Holy Ghost,
Paul bears them record that they have a zeal
of God. Still they were an unsaved people :
their desire to please God could not in itself
save them ; they could not be accepted simply
for their zeal's sake. Why not ? He tells us
—because their zeal was "*not according to knowledge.* They were seeking salvation, *but not
in God's way ;* and consequently, with all their
seeking, they had not found what they wanted.
What was their error ? The third and fourth
verses of the chapter are simple in their ex-
planation : "*For they being ignorant of God's
righteousness, and going about to establish their
own righteousness, have not submitted themselves to
the righteousness of God. For Christ is* THE END

OF THE LAW FOR RIGHTEOUSNESS *to every one that believeth.*" Here was their error : *and the fact that they were unsaved, proves that it was a* SOUL-DESTROYING ERROR. *They were ignorant of the righteousness which God in Christ has provided for His people ; they knew nothing of Christ, the end of the law* FOR RIGHTEOUSNESS, and so were seeking to please and propitiate God *by establishing a righteousness of their own.*

Now the sinner anxious about his soul is not called on to seek to propitiate God by a righteousness of his own, or in other words by a series of reformations and repentances, so that for these things' sake God may be favourably disposed towards him : this is what these unsaved Israelites did, and *is zeal, but not according to knowledge ;* but he is called upon, as the very first thing he does, to accept CHRIST,—*to begin with Him ;* and the moment he does so, he begins *not at the beginning,* but at *the end of the law, with all its requirements perfectly fulfilled and kept* FOR HIM ; and he has in Christ a righteousness for the sake of which in God's sight he appears unblameable, unreproveable, spotless : "Christ the end of the law *for righteousness* to every one that believeth."

Do you remember the Scripture which saith

"He" (that is, God) "hath made Him to be sin for us, who knew no sin, that we might be made *the righteousness of God* in Him"? (2 Cor. v. 21.) Now, did you ever ask yourself the question—how could Christ be made sin? He was the image of the invisible God; the brightness of His Father's glory; His Father's well-beloved Son, who did always those things which pleased Him; He knew no sin, neither was guile found in His mouth; *how then could He be made sin?* Only in the same way that *we can be made righteous.* By the transfer of our sins to Christ, God made Him who knew no sin, to be sin in His sight, that by the transfer of His righteousness to us, who knew no righteousness, we might be made righteous in His sight; and as it was ONLY by the imputation of sins not His own, that Jesus could by any possibility be made SIN, so is it only by the imputation of righteousness not his own, that the sinner can by any possibility be made RIGHTEOUS, AND SO PASSED GUILTLESS IN THE DAY OF JUDGMENT.

There is another thing I would observe before I leave this subject: namely, that a sinner cannot be saved *half in the righteousness which Christ is made unto him, and half in his own rigteousness.* He cannot keep what he considers the good bits of his life, and patch up the remainder with the gift of Christ.

I believe multitudes are perishing under the delusion that this is possible; they find it harder to part with *"righteous self"* than with *"sinful self."* They think that their life has not been altogether so bad as it might have been, and that for the sake of the good part God will forgive the bad part, and make up— not a whole righteousness, they do not think they require that—but *what they lack*, out of His mercies in Christ. Now there can be no greater deception or lie of the devil than this, *for he who depends in part or in whole on his own righteousness will surely be damned*. I write strongly. This truth is so important to be received that I can use no other word: *it is the truth of God*.

There are two righteousnesses in which a man can stand before God in judgment, and two only. The one is his own righteousness, and the other is Christ's righteousness; and he must choose which of these two it shall be. It must be *wholly* the one, however, or *wholly* the other; for we cannot stand *partly* in the one and *partly* in the other. The righteousness which is the gift of Christ,—that spotless robe, that wedding garment,—is like the vesture on

which the soldiers cast lots, without seam, and
woven throughout, and you cannot rend it.   It
is that perfect obedience by which St. Paul
says (Rom. v. 19), "*many shall be made righteous*," and is compounded of His thoughts, His
words, His works, while He was upon the
earth.   The righteousness of the creature is
compounded in the same way, and is made up
of his thoughts, his words, his works; and it
is *between these two that we are called upon to
choose.*   Renounce your own life altogether:
give it, as a garment spotted with the flesh—
all its fancied good bits, as well as its bad and
indifferent bits—just as it is, to Christ; and He
will accept it, cast it behind His back, and
remember it no more.   HE HAS ALREADY RE-
CEIVED WHAT IT DESERVED; and He will then
give you the gift of His righteousness, and YOU
SHALL RECEIVE WHAT IT DESERVES : but if you
appear before God in your own righteousness,
and that righteousness is one whit less perfect
than the righteousness which God at such a
cost to Himself has offered to you; if God, the
righteous Judge, is able to detect the least
difference between your righteousness and
Christ's, you will surely meet the fate of him
who came to the marriage supper without a
wedding-garment, and be cast into outer-dark-

ness, where there is weeping and wailing, and gnashing of teeth.

Nay more, I will go further, and say that even this righteousness would not save you, for you would still be guilty of rejecting CHRIST'S WORK, which is GOD'S WAY OF SALVATION.

X.

God's Way of Salvation.

The Blood of Christ.

AND now the three days have been accomplished; the lamb, fitting type of Him who was holy, harmless, undefiled, and separate from sinners, has been kept up for the time appointed; and the day has arrived that is to witness GOD'S JUDGMENT OF DEATH, HIS SALVATION BY BLOOD, AND THE DELIVERANCE OF HIS PEOPLE ISRAEL.

We read (Ex. xii. 21), "Then Moses called for all the elders of Israel, and said unto them, Draw out and take you a lamb according to your families, and kill the passover. And ye shall take a bunch of hyssop, and dip it in the blood that is in the bason, and strike the lintel and two side-posts with the blood that is in the bason; and none of you shall go out at the door of his house until the morning. For the Lord will pass through to smite the Egyptians; and when He seeth the blood upon the lintel, and on the two side-posts, the Lord will pass over the door, and will not suffer the destroyer to come in unto your houses to smite you. And the people bowed the head and worshipped. And the children of Israel went away, and did as the Lord had commanded Moses and Aaron.

"And it came to pass, that at midnight the Lord smote all the first-born in the land of Egypt, from the first-born of Pharaoh that sat on his throne unto the first-born of the captive that was in the dungeon; and all the first-born of cattle. And Pharaoh rose up in the night, he, and all his servants, and all the Egyptians: and there was a great cry in Egypt; for *there was not a house where there was not one dead!* And he called for Moses and Aaron by night, and said, Rise up, and get you forth from among my people, both ye and the children of Israel, and go, serve the Lord, as ye have said. Also take your flocks and your herds, as ye have said, and be gone; and bless me also. And the Egyptians were urgent upon the people, that they might send them out of the land in haste; for they said, We be all dead men!"

Fearful must have been the cry that was

raised that night in the land of Egypt! Through
the length and breadth of Pharaoh's wide do-
mains a corpse in every house! If we had
witnessed such a scene could we ever have
forgotten it? Doubtless we think not. Yet,
alas, alas! that I should be able to utter such
a truth, it only requires that our eyes should
be really opened to see reality as it is, and we
should every day see something not only very
like it, but far more terrible.

We read in the first Epistle to Timothy v. 6,
that—"She that liveth in pleasure is dead
while she liveth;" and in the first Epistle of
John v. 12, that—"He that hath not the Son
of God hath not life." Now if these two Scriptures, and the many others that give the same
testimony are true *(and they are true)*, are there
many houses through the length and breadth
of these dominions, in which there is not ONE
DEAD! With the greatest stretch of charity
can we think that there are many houses
in which there is not one inmate who is a
stranger to Jesus?—one inmate living to do that
which is right in his own eyes, without regard
to the commandments of God? I will not say
there are no such houses: God forbid. But let
us recollect that there is no middle position,—
that we are either alive unto God, or dead in

trespasses and sins; either we have the Son, and so have life; or we have not the Son of God, and so have not life; and I firmly believe that for every house where there is not one dead, there are hundreds where there is not merely one dead, but *where they are all dead together!*

Oh, how should this thought stir Christians! The day of grace for the first-born of Egypt had passed, and their death was irremediable. Not so the death of the dead ones amongst us. God's people possess a treasure in earthen vessels, even the incorruptible seed of His Holy Word, which can quicken these dead! God's Word, received by faith, can give them life; and *faith cometh by hearing.* (Rom. x. 17.) Oh, Christian brother, Christian sister, scatter the life-giving Word as you have opportunity! scatter it, scatter it, in season, out of season. The wind bloweth where it listeth, and if we obey the command to sow, we can set no limit to the blessing that may follow, but if we do not scatter the seed, there is nothing for the wind to blow; and if we are not helping God in His work He looks on us as hindering it. (Matt. xii. 30.)

The destroyer had smitten the Egyptians, but how is it that no Israelite is smitten?

Amongst the Egyptians there is one dead in every house! Amongst the Israelites there is not one dead! The judgment that had destroyed the one had not come near the other. How was this? You will at once say, and rightly say, "THE BLOOD!" *It was the Blood,* AND THE BLOOD ONLY, *that made the difference.* Death had been abroad, but under shelter of that blood the Israelites had rested safely. God had made known to them His way of salvation, and they had accepted it; and now the judgment has passed over, and they are saved, every one.

The commandment was, "*Strike the lintel and two side-posts with the blood; and none of you shall go out at the door of the house till the morning.*" The promise to obedience was, "*When I see the blood upon the lintel, and on the two side-posts, I will pass over the door, and will not suffer the destroyer to come in unto your houses to smite you.*" If any of them had doubted the efficacy of this blood, and so had neglected to sprinkle it; or if any had—no matter upon what plea— come from beneath its shelter, disobeying the command, "*None of you go out at the door of his house till the morning,*" his mere name of Israelite would have availed him nothing: he would have perished with the Egyptians. But these people believed God, and obeyed God, and *their faith was their salvation.*

What a mine of instruction is there in the few words in which the record of this saving faith is given! *Remember, it is recorded for our learning.* God said, "Take a lamb, slay it, sprinkle the blood upon the lintels and the door-posts of your houses; on no account come out from under the shelter of that blood till the night of judgment has passed over; and when I see the blood I will spare you." And how did the people receive the message? Did they cavil, or question, or ask explanations beyond what God had seen fit to give? Not one of them. In that vast assembly to whom were preached these glad tidings of "*salvation by blood*" no voice was heard either in doubt or argument, but the record of their saving faith is given us in these simple words: "THE PEOPLE BOWED THE HEAD AND WORSHIPPED— AND WENT AWAY, AND DID AS THE LORD HAD COMMANDED."

Oh, that every one who hears the Gospel would go away and do likewise! Nothing more is needed for the salvation of the very chief of sinners. A far more fearful judgment than any that befel Egypt is quickly hastening on this ungodly world; and unless we do as the Israelites did, our destruction is certain. We have all sinned—some in a greater, some in a less degree, if you like so to speak, but all sufficiently to bring us in guilty before God; and I have before shown you that no efforts of our own whatever—no prayers, no tears, no amendment of life—can ever atone for the least past transgression, or save us from the wages of sin at the day of judgment. But God has provided a way of salvation for us : and as it was to the Israelites, so it is to us,—SALVATION BY BLOOD. Many, in the present day, would try to explain away this doctrine ; but listen not to their teaching, if you would escape destruction. God has said (Heb. ix. 23), "Without shedding of blood there is no remission ; " and again (Lev. xvii. 11), "It is the blood that maketh an atonement for the soul." This is the teaching of all Scripture ; and let God be true, and every man a liar. As the passover was slain for these Israelites, and the blood of the Lamb was the only thing that saved them ; so Christ, our passover, has been sacrificed for us (1 Cor. v. 7) ; and *His blood is the only thing that can save us.* The Old Testament or Covenant was, "Keep my commandments and live;" but by this Old Testament no man could be saved, for no man could ever keep God's

commandments. But fifteen hundred years
after the children of Israel had slain the Paschal lamb, and by virtue of its blood had been
delivered from the destroyer,—on the same
month, and on the very same day of the month
(the 14th day of the month Abib), did the Lord
Jesus Christ eat the passover with His disciples:
and after supper He took the cup, and said, "*This
cup is* THE NEW TESTAMENT IN MY BLOOD, *which
is shed for you.*" (Luke xxii. 20.)

Blessed word! A New Testament! a better
Covenant! and established upon better promises. (Heb. viii. 6.) A covenant of which
Jesus Christ Himself is Mediator, and the conditions of which are written in HIS OWN BLOOD!
Conditions, did I say? There is but one; and
that is, that in child-like, simple faith, we accept
what God has given.

God so loved the world that He gave His
only-begotten Son, that whosoever believeth in
Him should not perish, but have everlasting
life: and no matter what he has been or what
he is, Christ, and Christ crucified, must be the
beginning of religion to every man: *until he
has begun here, he has not begun at all.*

"I delivered unto you *first of all,*" says Paul,
in his Epistle to the Corinthians, xv. 3, "that
which I also received, how that Christ died for

our sins." The first thing that brought to me
a sense of pardon and peace, when I, Paul, the
persecutor, blasphemer, and injurious, was led,
by the grace of God, to cry for mercy and forgiveness, was the first thing I preached to you.
And we learn from 1 Cor. vi., that through
faith in this Word preached, the very vilest
of sinners — fornicators, idolaters, adulterers,
thieves, covetous, drunkards, and others too
bad to mention—were washed, justified, sanctified in the name of the Lord Jesus, and by the
Spirit of our God. "Other foundation can no
man lay than that is laid, which is Jesus
Christ." (1 Cor. iii. 11.) We may build on
this foundation after it is laid, and of the greatest consequence it is to us to take care what we
do build; but until this is laid we have nothing
whereon to build—no foundation to support a
superstructure; and all our spiritual labour is
labour lost, labour in vain, because labour
OUT OF THE LORD.

Is it not the declaration of the Lord Himself,
—*I am the beginning?* Paul made Him the
beginning; and so must we, if we would be
saved. As well might a teacher commence
to teach a child B, and C, and D, and E, and
higher up in the rudiments of learning, before
he had taught him the first letter in the alpha-

bet, as for a spiritual instructor to direct a man's attention to any of the other truths of religion, until (by the grace of God) he had taught him to know the great Alpha, JESUS CHRIST, and to rest upon His blood.

I ask a man if he has got Christ, and he says "No!" I ask him again, Do you conside yourself then as altogether without religion? He says "No" again : *"I do not think I am quite so bad as that."*

Now these two answers are a contradiction, and cannot be true together; for either a man is utterly and totally without religion, or *he has Christ.* The man who has not Christ, has not God: and the man who has not God, may have a religion that may do to live with; yea, even a religion that may give him a false peace upon his death-bed: but he has no religion that can save him in the day of judgment from being cast soul and body into hell. On the other hand, the man who, by the power of the Holy Ghost, without attending to his own frames or feelings, but in simple dependence on the Word of God, takes Christ as He is offered to him in the Gospel, *has got salvation;* HE HAS GOT CHRIST, *and he is complete in Him.* (Colos. ii. 10.) *He has got a death to present to God instead of his death: a righteousness to supply his lack of righteousness: and the promise of the Holy Spirit to teach him all things, to deliver him from the power of sin, and to make him meet to be partaker of an inheritance with the saints in light.*

NOTHING can cleanse from sin but the blood of Jesus Christ: but the blood of Jesus Christ, God's Son, can cleanse from all sin; and how much sin has a man left on him after he is cleansed from ALL SIN? Oh, what glorious things are spoken of this blood! How it meets all the needs of the poor sinner. Until he has accepted it, he is described as *"without Christ, having no hope, and without God in the world."* (See Eph. ii. 12.) But no sooner does he do as the Israelites did,—receive in simple and unquestioning faith God's way of salvation,—than he who before was a stranger and afar off from God, is brought nigh by this blood of Christ. He is purchased with this blood. (Acts xx. 28; Eph. ii. 13.) He is washed in this blood. (Rev. i. 5.) He gets forgiveness through this blood. (Eph. i. 7.) He gets peace through this blood. (Colos. i. 20.) He is justified by this blood. (Rom. v. 9.) He is sanctified with this blood. (Heb. xiii. 12.) He has complete redemption through this blood. (Colos. i. 14.) And in that awful day, when like Joshua, the High Priest (Zech. iii. 1), the poor sinner stands before the angel of the Lord, with Satan at his right hand to resist him, THE LAMB SLAIN will be an answer sufficient for all that can be brought against him, and he shall overcome the accuser BY THIS BLOOD. (Rev. xii. 11.)

I surely need not stop to tell you that by the blood of Christ is meant the death of Christ. We have done things in God's judgment worthy of death, and our lives are justly forfeited to the law which we have broken : but Christ has died for the ungodly, and therefore—*and only therefore, and for no other reason whatever*—every ungodly sinner who accepts Jesus Christ, is looked upon by God as having in Christ *died already for his sins*, and God will never exact their penalty twice over. Christ has laid down His life already for the believer : and "the life of the flesh is in the blood : " and thus saith the Lord (Levit. xvii. 11), "I have given it to you upon the altar, to make an atonement for your souls ; for it is the blood that maketh an atonement for the soul."

One more word before I leave this part of my subject. The Israelites accepted God's way of salvation by blood, *and were saved*, before they took one step towards the land of Canaan. They had become dissatisfied with their position as the slaves of Pharaoh,—they had sighed by reason of their bondage, and they were willing (God helping them) to come out from Egypt long before they got out.

Now this dissatisfaction, and this sighing is the exact type of a mind prepared by the Holy Spirit *to receive God's way of salvation, but it was not that salvation itself. The blood was the salvation of the Children of Israel, and the blood only.* The desire for deliverance was rather the type of that repentance or change of mind of which our Lord and His disciples so often spake; and which, though not salvation itself, must take place in a man, or he cannot be saved: for it is written, "*Except ye repent, ye shall all likewise perish.*"

I introduce this subject here,—quite aware that it may appear forced, and out of its place, —because I believe many mistakes have gone abroad about this word repentance, and that many sincerely anxious and penitent souls in God's sight have been sore let and hindered in their search after salvation by a misapprehension of the meaning of the word.

Satan, if he cannot keep us altogether careless about our souls, endeavours to lead us astray by misinterpretations of Scripture, and unsound deductions from God's written Word.

And this is most glaringly his manner with the word repentance.

Μετανοία, the word in the original Greek, and which we translate "repentance," signifies literally, A CHANGE OF MIND; and the verse I have quoted from Luke xiii. 3, "*Except ye repent, ye shall all likewise perish*," would be as correctly—I might say even more correctly, because more literally translated,—if it had been, "Except *ye change your minds*, ye shall all likewise perish."

Divers as are the minds of men, and different as are their ideas of happiness, in one respect they are all alike. They none of them by nature look on THE LORD JEHOVAH as the greatest and chiefest good, but all seek their happiness in *something that is not* GOD. I have fully described the state of the natural man in the beginning of this little book, I shall not therefore repeat it; but will only say that, being born without God, and the slave of the spirit that he inherited from Adam, he is by nature *contented with his position;* and so long as his earthly condition is a prosperous one, it troubles him little that he is WITHOUT GOD. Now there must be *repentance*,—a change of mind about this, or we cannot be saved. The very first words our Saviour preached in public

were, "*Repent ye*, and believe the Gospel."
Peter's first teaching after our Lord's ascension
was the same: "*Repent* and be baptized every
one of you, in the name of Christ Jesus." And
Paul testified everywhere, "to the Jews and
also to the Greeks, *repentance towards God*, and
faith to our Lord Jesus Christ."

Now this repentance, preached so continually
by our Lord and His Apostles, is nothing more
or less than *a change of mind* that leads us
habitually to put *God first, and to desire and seek
Him before all things*. It is a change of mind that
works in us the desire to obey the first commandment, "THOU SHALT HAVE NONE OTHER
GODS BEFORE ME; *and without this, all professed
acceptance of Christ is a delusion, and not the work
of the Holy Spirit.*

There may, or there may not be, as an
accompaniment to true repentance, such a keen
sense of our past sinfulness as fills our eyes
with tears, and our hearts with known and felt
sorrow; but whether there is, or is not, this
sorrow is *not in itself repentance*, or even necessary to be experienced, before we may close
with Christ, and accept His salvation. If we
really desire God, *the very fact that we desire
Him* is a proof that our hearts are changed
towards Him; and it is the teaching of Satan

to stumble the anxious soul and to keep him in unbelief, that until he has felt *a certain amount of sensational sorrow about the heart*, he cannot be truly penitent, and must not appropriate the promises of Christ, or believe in the forgiveness of his sins. This is directly contrary to the teaching of the Bible, where the evidence of repentance is made to consist *in conduct;* a willingness and a determination to give up sin, and to obey at all costs the commandments of the Lord. A man who is conscious that he has this Spirit in him only requires FAITH IN THE WORD OF THE LORD to enrol himself amongst the blessed; for he is of the number of those who hunger and thirst after righteousness; and it is unbelief alone that can hinder him from resting in the promise that he "shall be satisfied."

As a rule, I think it is *after a man* has been enabled by God's Spirit to lay hold of Christ, and to realize on the faith of God's Word, that, in spite of all that he has been, and still is, his sins are forgiven him, and he is a saved man; that then it is, as he sits in some quiet solitude reflecting on the marvellous difference between being lost and saved, and on the marvellous love that sought him when he was lost, and found and saved him; that then it is,—love and peace at work together in his heart,—that the tears of godly sorrow run down his cheeks, deepening that "*repentance*" which first showed itself in a willingness to forsake sin, and strengthening that "*change of mind*" which first made him turn to God.

No man, however, can lay down an exact rule for these things. God is a Sovereign, and will bring His people to Himself, "*in the way that He shall choose.*" But this we do know,— that every one who confesseth and forsaketh sin, and believing in the Lord Jesus Christ, goes to God in His name, shall most certainly not be cast out, but shall be saved. He will not be saved, however, *because* of his repentance or change of mind; neither will he be saved *because* he confesses and forsakes his sin; he will not be saved even *because* he believes in the Lord Jesus, or *because* he goes to God in His name. Without these things it is most true that he will be lost; yet for all that, the only and alone procuring cause of his salvation is "THE BLOOD OF THE LAMB."

XI.

The Exodus.

The New Name.

LET us bear in mind then that the children
of Israel were saved BEFORE they took
one step out of the land of Egypt. They
listened to what God said, and considering
nothing else, obeyed Him and WERE SAVED.

But, being saved, what was their IMMEDIATE
conduct? How long did they remain in the
land after their salvation? A few days: a week
perhaps, or a month, to make their necessary
preparations? NOT ONE DAY! But on the very
same day—the day on which they were saved—
the day of the blood-sprinkling—without even
waiting to bake their bread—with "their dough
before it was leavened, their kneading-troughs
being bound up in their clothes upon their
shoulders,"—did these Israelites, about six hun-

dred thousand on foot that were men, with their children, and flocks, and herds, even very much cattle, go out from Egypt, and start on their wilderness journey, for the land of Canaan.

And as it was with them, so it must be, and so will it ever be, with him who truly receives God's way of salvation. Having been taught by the Holy Ghost to accept Christ, his body has become the temple of the living God; having fed by faith on the true Paschal Lamb, he HATH, as Jesus Himself tells us (John vi. 54—56), "EVERLASTING LIFE;" he dwelleth in Christ, and Christ in him—and the devil cannot for one moment keep him longer in his kingdom. As no thought, even for necessary food, could detain these Israelites in Egypt, so no earthly consideration can detain the true believer in the world. Satan is still in him, but the Holy Ghost is in him also; and it is the Holy Ghost who leads him now, and not Satan. Satan will still tempt, and harass, and strive to hinder—and, alas, even sometimes may gain a triumph; but he can no longer rule, and reign, and exercise dominion: a stronger than he has bound the strong man, and delivered "the lawful captive;" and the slave of Satan has become Christ's freedman, and is led by the

Spirit of God. *That leading is invariably the same* : OUT OF THE WORLD." (2 Cor. vi. 14—18.)

It is to be remarked also, that these Israelites, though they came out on the very day, not only did not, but *could not* get out of Egypt, until after their salvation. Before this they were anxious to get out, and in many ways they had proved it; and even God Himself had fought manifestly on their side, and against Pharaoh, to compel him to let them go : yet their anxieties and strivings and contendings had effected no deliverance. In spite of God and man, Pharaoh still held the Israelites in his power, bond-slaves in the land of Egypt.

But behold, from the moment that they fed on the Lamb slain, and trusted in the blood for their salvation, everything is changed. All things begin to work together for their good. Their leaving Egypt has now not only become easy, but actually a necessity; for the very Egyptians who had before suffered so many things rather than let them go, are now "urgent upon the people, that they might send them out of the land in haste," so "that they were thrust out of Egypt, and could not tarry." Neither do they go empty-handed. Who can tell the mighty power of God to us-ward who believe? He gave the people favour in the sight of the

Egyptians, and jewels of gold, and jewels of silver, and raiment, are freely lavished on them. In the night that they took the blood every difficulty vanished; and Israel, having spoiled the Egyptians, went with a high hand out of the land of Egypt. (Exod. xiv. 8.)

Surely he may run that readeth these lessons of the Holy Spirit. Neither good desires, nor prayers, nor wrestlings, nor strivings, nor any other thing but THE BLOOD OF CHRIST, can so bring us unto the power of God as TO ENABLE HIM to deliver us out of the power of Satan. The desires in the hearts of the Israelites to come out from Egypt, and the judgments on Pharaoh to compel him to let the people go, were doubtless both of them the work of God; and, doubtless, the desires, and prayers, and wrestlings of the sinner to escape from the power of Satan, are the strivings of the Holy Ghost within him, not willing that any should perish. But, as in the case of Pharaoh and the Israelites, if there had been no judgment of death, and no salvation by blood, they never would have been delivered; so in the case of the anxious sinner,—unless he ceases from his own experiences and believes in the Lord Jesus Christ, he never will be saved.

Moreover, it is a most solemn fact, that the

wrestlings and strivings of the Holy Ghost are
not only not salvation, but very often do not
end in it. In too many cases He is grieved,
and put away, and finally quenched. The
words of Stephen to the Jewish rulers may
be addressed with truth to multitudes : " Ye
stiffnecked, in heart and ears ye do always
resist the Holy Ghost." And there are many
doubtless at this moment amongst the lost,
whose damning sin was that THEY QUENCHED
THE SPIRIT. (1 Thess. v. 19.) We have no
salvation until we close with Jesus. However
strong our convictions, or excellent our moral
character, we are in our sins till then, and
without God in the world : but the instant we
receive Christ, His Father becomes our Father,
and His God our God ; and He is able to
accomplish both for us, and in us, all His
mighty purposes of mercy.

I would say it very reverently, but I am sure
it is a most Scriptural truth, that until the
sinner believes in Jesus Christ, God has NO
POWER TO SAVE HIM. Christ is " THE POWER OF
GOD UNTO SALVATION : " God's " INVENTION,"
if I may so speak,—called in Scripture, " THE
WISDOM OF GOD," for the salvation of sinners.
And had there been *any other way* in which He
could have been a "just God and a Saviour,"

He would have spared His only begotten Son: but there was *no other way*, and so God freely gave Him up for us all; and *in this way* He is able to save to the uttermost them that come to God by Him.

Oh, what false hopes and refuges of lies about God's mercy would be swept away, if but this truth was fully recognised,—that OUT OF CHRIST, or unless WE BELIEVE IN CHRIST, which is the same thing, God has no POWER to save us. How plainly does the New Testament speak on this subject : Jesus COULD DO no mighty work in His own country, because of their unbelief. (Matt. xiii. 58, and Mark vi. 5.) And how easily might this be understood, if men would but take the trouble to think.

There are but *two powers* on earth,—the Lord Jesus Christ and Satan ; both these are striving to do a mighty work,—the one to save, the other to destroy the sinner; and he that the sinner BELIEVES, be it Christ or Satan, does the mighty work that he desires. The other, *he that is not believed*, cannot do it, simply *because he is not believed*. The Lord Jesus Christ says, Believe in my Word, and I will save you. Instantly another spirit rises up, and says something, which however plausible it may sound, contradicts that word : if we believe that spirit, Christ cannot do His mighty work in us, *because we will not believe Him;* we believe the spirit that contradicts Him, and so make God a liar. But if we say to this spirit,—no matter how he approaches us, whether he comes as a power of darkness, or an angel of light; whether it be through the evidence of our feelings, or fears, or wisdom, or senses,—*Show me what you tell me in the Bible;* and if when he cannot, we reply to him in the words of Jesus, "Get thee behind me, Satan; for thou savourest not the things that be of God;" then this spirit cannot do his mighty work in us, *because we will not believe him.*

Oh, the mighty power of unbelief! By faith we resist the devil, and drive him from us, so that he cannot harm us; by unbelief we resist the Holy Spirit, and drive Him from us, so that He cannot save us. How earnestly should we pray, "Lord, grant me that faith which faileth not: Lord, increase in me true faith continually."

There is one expression that occurs twice in the last few verses of this wonderful twelfth chapter of Exodus, to which, before I conclude my observations upon it, I would request your special notice. It is the new name given by God to the children of Israel. "THE HOSTS OF THE LORD!" "THE ARMIES OF ISRAEL!"

Thus we read: "Now the sojourning of the children of Israel, who dwelt in Egypt, was four hundred and thirty years. And it came to pass at the end of the four hundred and thirty years, even the self-same day it came to pass, that all the hosts of the Lord went out from the land of Egypt. It is a night to be much observed unto the Lord for bringing them out from the land of Egypt. The Lord did bring the children of Israel out of the land of Egypt by their armies."

Wonderful words! Hosts of the Lord! Soldiers! and soldiers composing the armies of the living God!

And who are these hosts? who are the soldiers that compose these armies, and that are honoured with such noble titles? They are the CHILDREN OF ISRAEL! "The Lord did bring THE CHILDREN OF ISRAEL out by their armies."

It is most true! The very same children of Israel who but a little while ago were in the horrible pit and the miry clay—slaves to Pharaoh and the Egyptians; the very same who, but a little while ago, were set to the impossible service of making bricks without straw, and who, because they failed, were beaten; the same, in short, who, but a little while ago, were the type of all that was hopeless and degraded,—these children of Israel cried unto the Lord, and He sent them His Word, and declared to them His way of salvation: they believed it, and acted on it; and in that instant,—not the next day, or a week, or a month afterwards, but "on the very same night,"—from the most abject amongst men, they were at once exalted to the noblest place amongst the nations. From slaves they became soldiers, and not soldiers merely, but soldiers of the living God,—hosts of the Lord Almighty, commissioned to fight His battles, under the banner of the Lord of hosts, their Leader!

What we are, what we may be: OURSELVES —A PICTURE.

XII

The Destruction. The Deliverance.

LET us now go on to the fourteenth chapter of this Book of Exodus. We read,—

"And it was told the king of Egypt that the people fled: and the heart of Pharaoh and of his servants was turned against the people; and they said, Why have we done this, that we have let Israel go from serving us? And he made ready his chariot, and took his people with him: and he took six hundred chosen chariots of Egypt, and captains over every one of them. And he pursued after the children of Israel, and overtook them encamping by the sea. And when Pharaoh drew nigh, the children of Israel lifted up their eyes, and behold the Egyptians marched after them; and they were sore afraid: and the children of Israel cried out unto the Lord. And the Lord said unto Moses, Wherefore criest thou unto Me?— Speak unto the childrn of Israel, that they go forward.

"And the angel of God, which went before the camp of Israel, removed and went behind them : and the pillar of the cloud went from before their face, and stood behind them : and it came between the camp of the Egyptians and the camp of Israel; and it was a cloud and darkness to them, but it gave light by night to these : so that the one came not near the other all the night.

"And Moses stretched out his hand over the sea; and the Lord caused the sea to go back by a strong east wind all that night, and made the sea dry land, and the waters were divided. And the children of Israel went into the midst of the sea upon the dry ground : and the waters were a wall unto them on their right hand and on their left.

"And the Egyptians pursued, and went in after them to the midst of the sea, even all Pharaoh's horses, his chariots, and his horsemen. And it came to pass that in the morning watch the Lord looked unto the host of the Egyptians through the pillar of fire and of the cloud, and troubled the host of the Egyptians, and took off their chariot wheels, that they drave them heavily : so that the Egyptians said, Let us flee from the face of Israel; for the Lord fighteth for them against the Egyptians.

"And the Lord said unto Moses, Stretch out thine hand over the sea, that the waters may come again upon the Egyptians, upon their chariots, and upon their horsemen. And Moses stretched forth his hand over the sea, and the sea returned to his strength when the morning appeared: and the Egyptians fled against it; and the Lord overthrew the Egyptians in the midst of the sea. And the waters returned, and covered the chariots, and the horsemen, and all the host of Pharaoh that came into the sea after them; there remained not so much as one of them. But the children of Israel walked upon dry land in the midst of the sea; and the waters were a wall unto them on their right hand, and on their left.

"Thus the Lord saved Israel that day out of the hand of the Egyptians; and Israel saw the Egyptians dead upon the sea-shore."

Oh, what a mass of instruction is here, and all written for our learning! First, what was the destruction of Pharaoh? HIS LAST SIN. A man's last sin is always his destruction. No amount of past guilt, be you who or what you may, will ever destroy your soul, if you will NOW confess and forsake your sins, and go to God by Jesus Christ; but *beware of rejecting the present moment, or returning " again unto folly."*

God had visited Pharaoh in judgment, until he was brought not merely to promise, but actually to act as God had commanded him. And had he then really sought the Lord and taken Him for his God, the past would have been forgiven, and the day on which he let the children of Israel go would have been to him, as it was to them, *the beginning of days.* But no, the judgment was no sooner past than it was forgotten, and the old lust returned; and behold the man who had not only cried, "I have sinned, entreat the Lord for me," but who had given evidence of his repentance by giving up his sin; that man, let alone by God, and led captive by Satan at his will, *goes after his old sin again.*

Again: I would point out to you, as I did in the earlier chapters of this little book, what multitudes there are, apparently now hardened from the love and fear of God, who have done just the same. They were once in trouble, and they prayed, and promised, and vowed vows unto the Lord. They did more. They not only determined to forsake sin, but actually did give up much outward evil, and were made professedly willing to let all go that stood between their souls and God. And God heard their prayers and removed their trials, that He might prove what was in their hearts. How have they acted? Instead of performing their vows "it is happened unto them according to the true proverb: the dog is turned to his own vomit again, and the sow that was washed, to her wallowing in the mire." (2 Pet. ii. 22.)

Thus did Pharaoh, and thus did he again and again; and thus did he once too often, as does every lost man and woman with whom the Spirit strives. This going again after the Israelites filled up the measure of his iniquity.

It was his crowning sin, and God cut him down in it. Oh, reader, if you are still unsaved, tempt Him not to cut you down by resisting the lesson taught you. Again I say, no matter how much you have backslidden, mercy is still freely offered you, and pardon is within your reach; but as you would escape even a worse fate than that of Pharaoh, trifle not with the present moment, but at once go to Him who has written a special prayer for the backslider, and beseech Him to heal your backslidings for Jesus Christ's sake. (See Hosea xiv.)

Again: as the experience of Pharaoh is the experience of many of the lost, so is the experience of the Israelites (their old enemies coming after them again, and making them afraid) the experience of many of God's people. We read,

"the children of Israel lifted up their eyes,
and behold the Egyptians marched after them,
and they were sore afraid;" and I believe that
Satan sometimes successfully uses the fear of
this experience not only to make God's people
fearful, but as a means of keeping his own
people still under his bondage. How often do
such suggestions as these arise in the wavering
soul: " What is the use of my trying to be
religious ? What is the use of my going to
God and pleading the blood of Jesus Christ,
and praying for the Holy Spirit ? Do I not
know that very soon (perhaps before to-morrow
or even to-day is over) my old sins will be
besetting me again, and I shall be sure to be
overcome ?"

Now, to whom is a man listening when he
yields to such arguments ? To whom were
these Israelites listening, when they were sore
afraid, and said, " We shall die in the wilderness " ? You know very well who it was; and
you know very well, if such thoughts are in
your heart, who it is that is putting them there.
It is the spirit that this generation of Israelites
afterwards believed to their destruction. *It is
the spirit that makes God a liar*.

Had not God said, "I will bring you in," as
well as "bring you out"? And has not the

same God said to all under this dispensation who put their trust in Him, "*Sin shall not* have dominion over you: " and when God says "*it shall not*," will you dare to say "*it shall, and will*"? Is it not in dependence *on His promises* that we are to start on our Christian journey? Are we called to go a warfare on our own charges, or to fight our enemies in our own strength? It was for our sakes, for our learning, as well as for the trial of their faith, that these Israelites were brought into the position that we are now considering.

And truly, for flesh and blood the position was a trying one. Before them the Red Sea—behind them their old enemies, Pharaoh and the Egyptians. What was to be done? Would not Satan suggest that if they followed the leading of God, the very first step would be destruction? that it was better to return to Egypt; that slavery was preferable to death? Oh, never be deterred from entering on a religious life, because your own senses tell you that the very first step will be destruction. It is one of the most common devices of our great enemy. By God's grace, these children of Israel were not deterred. Their faith wavered, but it failed not: they had doubts and fears, but "his you are to whom you yield yourself servant to obey;" and they obeyed not the doubts and fears, but they obeyed the word of God: that word was—"GO FORWARD!"

"And the Lord said unto Moses, Speak unto the children of Israel, that they go forward."

"GO FORWARD." "To do so," says nature, "is certain death. There is the Red Sea before us, and we shall be drowned: *we must be.* In some cases it might be a matter of doubt, but in this case there is no doubt: to go forward is immediate and absolute destruction." "Very well," says faith: "so let it be. It is quite clear that God DOES SAY, 'Go forward;' and if we walk in the way of His commandments, we have the promise, 'Nothing shall in anywise harm us.' If to go forward is destruction, then destruction is the best thing that can happen to us; and if destruction is not the best thing that can happen to us, then we shall not be destroyed in going forward." Thus argued nature, and thus answered faith; and, thanks be to God, the Israelites walked by faith. They obeyed God, and *went forward.* What happened? Did they all perish? We have the account from God Himself: "Moses stretched out his hand over the sea; and the Lord caused the sea to go back by a strong east wind all that night, and made the sea dry land, and

the waters were divided. And the children of
Israel went into the midst of the sea upon the
dry ground : and the waters were a wall unto
them on their right hand, and on their left.''

And have such experiences as these been
confined to the Israelites of the days of Moses?
Where is the Christian of any standing who
cannot tell of many such! Yea, I believe they
are well known even to the very youngest
Christian. Which of us has not fancied, at
some time or another, that to go forward in
the direct way of God's commandments would
entail on us something very ruinous? Yet,
having gone forward, have we found it so?
Not once only, but again and again, has not
the thing we dreaded proved, like Bunyan's
chained lion, powerles to hurt us? If this
has not been your experience, reader, your experience has been different from mine; though
be sure of this, let that be as it may,—if you are
believing on the Lord Jesus Christ, all things
ARE working together for your good, and ''nothing shall by any means harm you.'' Still I
think that if you are God's child our experience
has been much the same ; and that you and I,
and multitudes can testify at this moment, that
having gone forward in the face of difficulty
and danger, we have found not only the diffi-

culty vanish and the danger no danger at all;
but the very line of conduct, which before by
faith we entered on it looked so ruinous and
destructive, has proved to us what going forward proved to these Israelites,—the very best
step for their own interests they ever took in
their lives.

Yet, alas, how sad it is that being able to set
to our seals that this is true of the past, we
should still be so weak in faith, and *backward
to go forward*. "Lord, increase our faith."

We must remember, however, that the promises, "All things work together for good,"
and "Nothing shall by any means harm you,"
are promises made only to the Israel of God,
or in other words to the true believer. I was
going to say that there are no promises in
Scripture, except to believers; but that is not
so; for there is an awful class of promises
made to the ungodly: still it is a most solemn
truth that the things that work together for
good to Christians, and are a savour of life
unto life to them, are a savour of death unto
death to others. Thus was it at the Red Sea.

We read, "The children of Israel went
into the midst of the sea upon the dry ground;
and the Egyptians pursued and went in after
them, even all Pharaoh's horses, his chariots,

and his horsemen." Poor, infatuated Pharaoh:
infatuated Egyptians. Thinking of no consequences, intent only on the gratification of
their immediate lusts and longings, King and
people rushed madly, blindly, presumptuously
(as many in our own day do to the Lord's
table and other Christian ordinances), along
the same path that had been opened by God
as a channel of salvation for His own people.
What a judgment followed!

No doubt you remember that the Lord, who
"went *before* the children of Israel by day in
a pillar of a cloud to lead them the way, and
by night in a pillar of fire to give them light,"
removed, when Pharaoh pursued the people,
and went *behind them;* and the pillar of cloud
came *between* the camp of the Egyptians and
the camp of Israel. First, went the Israelites,
then came the pillar of fire and of the cloud,
and then came the host of the Egyptians. And
it came to pass, that in the morning watch,
*when they were somewhere in the middle of the Red
Sea*, that "THE LORD LOOKED UNTO THE HOST
OF THE EGYPTIANS THROUGH THE PILLAR OF
FIRE AND OF THE CLOUD, AND TROUBLED THE
HOST OF THE EGYPTIANS."

"THE LORD LOOKED UNTO THE HOST OF THE
EGYPTIANS," and the look, we read, TROUBLED

THEM. No doubt it did; but what language can express that trouble! Dear, reader, whoever you are, think for a moment what must have been the feelings of Pharaoh when he saw that EYE OF GOD upon him. A beloved mother now in glory, first drew my attention to this portion of Scripture when I was a child, and I have never forgotten it. It was the first time that Pharaoh had ever seen God. He had no faith; he had walked by sight, and not by faith, and he had never seen Him who is Invisible. His own words, in reply to a message from this very God, had been, "I know not the Lord." But now Pharaoh saw God. It pleased God to manifest Himself visibly to Pharaoh. Pharaoh saw the Eye of God looking at Him,—and IT TROUBLED HIM!

Oh, reader, if YOU saw the Eye of God looking at YOU, would it trouble you? It is looking at YOU, whether you see it or not; and if you have not turned to Him already, if you will turn to Him now He will see you turn, and will accept you; but if not the day will come when you will see the Eye of God on you as Pharaoh saw it. You will see it on YOU IN JUDGMENT! This was Pharaoh's day of judgment. Pharaoh never saw God until the day of judgment: and better would it be for any

man never to have been born, that never to
see God till then.

God had been as close to Pharaoh all his life
as He was in that awful passage in the midst
of the Red Sea: and it was not because He
was so far off from him that Pharaoh had not
seen God; but Pharaoh, like all the rest of us,
had been born blind, and his eyes had never
been opened to see spiritual persons and spiritual
things; but now they are opened, as every man's
eyes will be opened, either here or hereafter,
and HE SAW GOD.

Again, I beseech you try and picture to yourself his feelings. Over and over again should
God's dealings have led him to repentance;
but that which should have softened him, only
made his heart the harder, and now his day of
grace was gone. Suddenly, in the very middle
of his sin, and without a possibility of escape,
he is brought face to face with God. We may
judge something of his agony from the cry it
wrung from him: "LET US FLEE."

"Let us flee." Whither can a man flee from
God? If he climb up into heaven, He is there;
if he make his bed in hell, He is there also.
There was a day once when Pharaoh might
have fled, not indeed from God, but to God,
and God would have been a Refuge for him;

but mercy and judgment had been alike in vain: nothing could either draw him or drive him to God; now God had risen up, and shut to the door of escape, and whither could he flee?

Poor, wretched Pharaoh! To him was fulfilled one of the promises made to the impenitent and unbelieving: "Because I have called, and ye refused; I have stretched out my hand, and no man regarded; but ye have set at nought all my counsel, and would none of my reproof: I will also laugh at your calamity; I will mock when your fear cometh." (Prov. i. 24—26.)

"Let us flee." It was too late. There was no place for repentance now for Pharaoh or his people. Moses stretched forth his hand over the sea, and the sea returned to its strength, and the Egyptians fled against it, and the Lord overthrew the Egyptians in the midst of the sea." Of all the host of Pharaoh that came into the sea after them, there remained not so much as one of them. "Thus the Lord saved Israel that day out of the hands of the Egyptians, and Israel saw the Egyptians dead upon the sea shore."

Reader, it was too late for Pharaoh, but it is not too late for you. Will you now, this moment, if you are yet an unsaved person, give up you sins, and flee to God, through Jesus Christ? *Answer the question to God, for it is He who asks it, and He is waiting for your answer.*

But you say you are already safe amongst the Israelites. Then by grace are you saved, through faith. Give God the glory, for it is He alone who has made you to differ.

XIII.

The Song of Praise. The Bitter Water.

"THEN sang Moses and the children of Israel this song unto the Lord, and spake, saying,

"I will sing unto the Lord, for He hath triumphed gloriously: the horse and his rider hath He thrown into the sea.

"The Lord is my strength and song, and He is become my salvation: He is my God, and I will prepare Him an habitation; my father's God, and I will exalt Him.

"The Lord is a man of war; the Lord is His name.

"Pharaoh's chariots and his host hath He cast into the sea: his chosen captains also are drowned in the Red Sea.

"The depths have covered them; they sank into the bottom as a stone.

" Thy right hand O Lord, is become glorious in power: Thy right hand hath dashed in pieces the enemy.

"And in the greatness of Thine excellency Thou hast overthrown them that rose up against Thee: Thou sentest forth Thy wrath, which consumed them as stubble.

"And with the blast of Thy nostrils the waters were gathered together, the floods stood upright as an heap, and the depths were congealed in the heart of the sea.

" The enemy said, I will pursue, I will overtake, I will divide the spoil; my lust shall be satisfied upon them; I will draw my sword, my hand shall destroy them.

" Thou didst blow with Thy wind, the sea covered them: they sank as lead in the mighty waters.

" Who is like unto Thee, O Lord, among the gods? who is like Thee, glorious in holiness, fearful in praises, doing wonders?

"Thou stretchest out Thy right, hand the earth swallowed them.

"Thou, in Thy mercy, hast led forth the people which Thou hast redeemed; Thou hast guided them in Thy strength unto Thy holy habitation.

" The people shall hear and be afraid: sorrow shall take hold on the inhabitants of Palestina.

"Then the dukes of Edom shall be amazed? the mighty men of Moab, trembling shall take hold upon them; all the inhabitants of Canaan shall melt away.

"Fear and dread shall fall upon them; by the greatness of Thine arm they shall be as still as a stone; till Thy people pass over, O Lord, till the people pass over, which Thou hast purchased.

"Thou shalt bring them in, and plant them in the mountain of Thine inheritance, in the place, O Lord, which Thou hast made for Thee to dwell in, in the sanctuary, O Lord, which Thy hands have established.

"The Lord shall reign for ever and ever."

Oh, what a song of praise is this which burst from the lips of these delivered Israelites! How magnificent in its language! How strong in its expressions of gratitude and faith! How full and clear in ascribing to God all the honour of their deliverance! Oh, how their hearts beat with love to Him, and how loudly, and in what grateful language did they express it.

And well they might. Would not you, if you had been in their situation, have sung the same song with the same feelings? Doubtless you think you would. Who could have done otherwise? What a miracle God had wrought for them! What a deliverance He had effected! But a little ago, and their only choice seemed between death and a return to Egypt. Now, the Red Sea rolled between them and Egypt, and their old task-masters lay dead upon its shore!

Let us, however, look a little deeper into the matter, for I believe there is a most instructive lesson to be learned from this song of praise. I do not believe these first words which burst so impulsively from the lips of this saved multitude were dictated by true love to God. We know indeed there were some amongst the people whose hearts were right with Him. Moses, who, inspired by God's Spirit, composed the song, and others (a remnant according to the election of grace) no doubt loved Him truly, for God in no age and in no nation where His name is named, has ever left Himself without a witness; but with very few exceptions these Israelites were self-deceivers, and had not the love of God in their hearts. They were not hypocrites: it is not necessary to be a hypocrite to be a self-deceiver: they did not know they did not love God,—they thought they did love Him,—they were

sure they did. Their own feelings told them
that they did, and they believed their feelings;
but they mistook that for love which was but *an
emotional sensation produced by exciting causes.*

Now I have witnessed the same effect from
the same style of cause, again and again; and
because *such things are so*, how closely should
we examine the foundation of our love to God.
I have seen persons who in the greatest stretch
of charity I could not believe to be Christians,
actually go down upon their knees when some
temporal mercy or blessing had been granted
them, and thank God for His goodness, with
the tears of joy and gratitude streaming down
their cheeks.

Now had any one gone to these Israelites on
the banks of the Red Sea, or to such a person
as I speak of as he arose from his knees, and
said, "I do not think you really love God,"
what would they have answered? Fully persuaded of it themselves, how vehement would
have been their asseverations. Not love God!
Yes, that I do! How can I help loving Him?
Has He not saved me out of all my troubles?
But for Him what should I be now? I thought
there was no hope for me,—that I was completely lost and ruined: but He has not only
delivered me out of all my difficulties, but my

future looks bright and happy. Not love Him!
I love Him dearly, and will bless and thank
Him as long as I live.

Some such as this would no doubt have been
their answer, and it would have been said in
sincerity; and I am prepared to admit that
there was not an Israelite in that camp on the
Red Sea who did not believe from the very
bottom of his treacherous and deceitful heart,
that he loved God. *They all felt it,* and there-
for they believed it : but what gave rise to
this sensational feeling of love?

The dispensation of God at the moment was
what these people liked. The order of His
dealings was in accordance with their own
desires. Their inclinations and His will concerning them agreed together. They had been
in a great temporal difficulty, and God had
effected for them a great temporal deliverance.
This called up the love they had, and filled
their hearts with joy and gladness. They felt
thankful to Him *for doing what they liked,* and
loudly sung His praises. But what was this
love worth when the Lord proved it? The
very same chapter (the 15th of Exodus) that
records their song of praise, records also that
in three days the very men who sang it murmured at God's dispensations, because, in the

leadings of His providence He gave them some
bitter water!

Thus we read: "Moses brought Israel from
the Red Sea, and they went out into the wilderness of Shur, and they went three days in
the wilderness and found no water. And when
they came to Marah they could not drink of
the waters of Marah, for they were bitter; and
the people murmured!" And in the next verse
we read: "There He *proved them.*"

He proved them; proved the reality of their
profession, as He will prove every man's. He
proved them by putting into their hands a
cup of bitter water, and they murmured! Oh,
does it not make us blush for human nature?
How great had been their deliverance! how
insignificant was the trial! The deliverance so
great, even in the eyes of God Himself, that
He has condescended to take from it one of
His own noblest titles: "*The Lord thy God
who brought thee out of the land of Egypt, and
out of the house of bondage.*" And the trial,
how insignificant! at the most a cup of bitter
water. Yet it was the same God and the
same Israelites. The God that gave the
bitter water was the God that gave the deliverance; the Israelites that murmured were
the Israelites that sang the song of praise

when they saw all their enemies dead upon the shore.

What we are : OURSELVES—A PICTURE! Who can deny the likeness? Has not every believer been saved from a far greater destruction than that from which these Israelites were delivered? And yet were is the saved man who is not compelled to confess that in his heart at least, if not with his lips, he has again and again murmured, when God has proved him with bitter water.

Beloved, these things should not be, and let us watch and pray hereafter that they may not be, for *they greatly dishonour God*. It is the same God who led the Israelites through the Red Sea, and to the bitter water, that first led us to Himself, and has since led us exactly to where we are; and if we have intrusted ourselves to Him, all our matters are ordered by Him, and when we murmur, we murmur against Him. Does He not love us, and does He not know what is best for us? Oh, for grace to remember, not only when His dispensations are agreeable to the flesh, but also when they are painful and flesh-crucifying, that the Lord reigneth, that the Lord is our Father, and to praise the Lord.

I believe there is nothing that honours God

more, or that God more honours, than praising
Him in tribulation; and few men know what a
talent He committs to their charge when He
gives them bitter water.   When did Paul ever
honour God more than when at midnight, in
the inner prison, his back cut to pieces by the
Roman whips, and his feet made fast in the
stocks, he prayed, and sang praises unto God?
And when did God ever honour Paul more
than when, through the instrumentality of
those prayers and praises, he brought the jailer
to his feet with the question, "What shall I do
to be saved?"   Paul was caught up into the
third heaven, and he thanked and praised God
for the honour and the glory.   Yet I never
heard of anybody who was converted by that
portion of Paul's history; but who can count
the numbers that owe their soul's salvation to
the answer given to the jailer's question—
"Believe on the Lord Jesus Christ, and thou
shalt be saved!"   *We never should have had that
Scripture if Paul had murmured in the inner prison
instead of singing praises.*

Job said, "The Lord gave and the Lord hath
taken away: blessed be the name of the Lord."
And the Lord said, "*In all this Job sinned not.*"
Job said, "Shall we receive good at the hand
of God, and shall we not receive evil?"   And

the Lord said, "*In all this did not Job sin with his lips*." Twice in ten verses it is recorded of Job, by the Holy Ghost, that he acted, when tried, so that God could and did say of him, "In all this did not Job sin." As far as I know, such a testimony was never vouchsafed to any other human being,—the Man Christ Jesus alone excepted. And God thus honoured Job, because Job honoured God and blessed Him in his affliction. (See Job i. 22, and ii. 10.)

God's commandment to His people is—"Give thanks for all things:" "Be content with such things as you have." God's promise is—"I will never leave you, nor forsake you." And the more literally we obey his commandments and rest on His promises, the more we prove our love to Him, and the more may we expect Him to manifest His love to us. And it is not at the waters of Marah only, but *because I never find these Israelites praising God for anything they did not like*, that I judge them as I do, and say that they mistook love of self for love of God. The publicans and sinners would have praised God on the shores of the Red Sea; not to have done so would have been *unnatural;* but the true Israelite, the man who really loved God, would have praised Him also at the waters of Marah.

And now, God having shown them what is in themselves,—sin and self-deception; shows them what is in Himself,—love and power. Love, not to deal with them after their sins, and power to make sweet the bitter water. Moses, we read, "cried unto the Lord, and the Lord showed him a tree, which when he had cast into the waters, the waters were made sweet." Moreover, he brought them on "to Elim, where were twelve wells of water, and threescore and ten palm-trees." Oh, how happy they were then, and doubtless again thought and felt that they loved God.

Reader, *love is a conduct, not a feeling;* and the evidence of love is *not emotion, but obedience.* (John xiv. 21—23.)

Is God proving you with bitter waters? "Behold the MAN, whose name is the BRANCH." (Zechariah vi. 12.) He can give you patience under your sufferings, and a happy issue out of all your afflictions.

XIV.

No Bread. No Water.

AND now God, having rested and refreshed the children of Israel at Elim, again leads them onward and forward towards the land of Canaan. Fresh trials overtake them, however, before they have gone far; and I believe no child of God ever yet escaped their next temptation. I do not say that it has succeeded, even for a moment, with every Christian; but I believe every Christian knows the temptation well. Our precious Lord Himself was subjected to it, and the disciple is not above his Master. It is this: "I shall perish in the wilderness for want of food."

On the fifteenth day of the second month after their departure from the land of Egypt, the children of Israel had no bread; and in the next chapter we learn also that they had no water.

Now, we cannot but confess that these were

hard trials, and according to all human calculation they rendered their position hopeless.
But surely the children of Israel have by this
time learned that they have nothing to do with
human calculations; they will look, not to their
position, but to their God; and calling to remembrance Egypt, the Red Sea, Marah, Elim,
—will go forward with unfailing faith, antici-
pating the Psalmist, and singing, " *The Lord is
my Shepherd, I shall not want.*"

So we should have thought, and so would
these Israelites have thought at the waters of
Elim; but alas, for poor human nature, if left
to itself, how sure to fall! The Israelites, tried
again and tempted, sinned again and doubted;
and instead of trusting, murmured.

Thus we read in the sixteenth of Exodus:
"And they took their journey from Elim, and
all the congregation of the children of Israel
came unto the wilderness of Sin, which is between Elim and Sinai, on the fifteenth day of the
second month after their departing out of the
land of Egypt. And the whole congregation
of the children of Israel murmured against
Moses and Aaron in the wilderness: and the
children of Israel said unto them, Would to
God we had died by the hand of the Lord in
the land of Egypt, when we sat by the flesh

pots, and when we did eat bread to the full; for ye have brought us forth into this wilderness, to kill this whole assembly with hunger." (Exod. xvi. 1—3.)

Again, in the beginning of the next chapter, we read: "And all the congregation of the children of Israel journeyed from the wilderness of Sin, after their journeys, according to the commandment of the Lord, and pitched in Rephidim: and there was no water for the people to drink. Wherefore the people did chide with Moses, and said, Give us water that we may drink. And Moses said unto them, Why chide ye with me? wherefore do ye tempt the Lord? And the people thirsted there for water; and the people murmured against Moses, and said, Wherefore is this that thou hast brought us up out of Egypt, to kill us and our children and our cattle with thirst?" (Ex. xvii. 1—3.)

"And Moses said, The Lord heareth your murmurings which ye murmur against Him: and what are we? Your murmurings are not against us, but against the Lord." (Ex. xvi. 8.)

Now it is particularly to be observed that the sin of which the children of Israel were on this occasion guilty was not in wishing for bread and water, but in thinking for one mo-

ment that after the Lord had brought them out
of Egypt He would suffer them, for the lack of
any needful thing, to come short of Canaan.
It was no sin to be hungry and thirsty; it was
a necessity of their nature. There is nothing
living that does not desire and require food:
when we do not, we are dead: and that they
did so was no sin. Their sin was *to doubt
either that God could or would support them in the
wilderness,—or allow those who followed His leadings to lack any good thing.* This was their sin.

It is just the same with the Christian now.
These Israelites did not more literally require
a supply of daily food for their bodies, than
does the Christian for his soul. Not to do so
is a sign of death, and the living soul would
soon die without it. And so far from its being
a sin, our Lord has pronounced that man
blessed who hungers and thirsts after righteousness, adding the most precious promise, that all
such shall be satisfied. But it is sin, and very
great sin, should this food not be perceptibly,
and to the evidence of our own senses, immediately supplied, to murmur and be fearful.
It was for *the trial of their faith* that these
things happened to the Israelites, as do the
trials of all Christians in all ages: and it is
"after ye have suffered awhile" that ye may

expect to be stablished, strengthened, settled. Thus it was that Moses, at the end of his ministry, interpreted the many mysterious dealings of God with Israel; and thus it is that I would urge on all who are striving to follow the leadings of His Spirit, to interpret dispensations which they do not understand.

"The way," says Moses, in the eighth of Deuteronomy, "which the Lord thy God led thee these forty years in the wilderness, was *to humble thee, and to prove thee, to know what was in thine heart, whether thou wouldst keep His commandments, or no. And He humbled Thee, and suffered thee to hunger, and fed thee with manna, which thou knewest not, neither did thy fathers know; that He might make thee know that man doth not live by bread only, but by every word that proceedeth out of the mouth of the Lord doth man live.*"

Now, in this Scripture it has pleased God to reveal for our learning why it was that He led these Israelites where He knew they would be tempted: *to humble them, to prove them, and to know what was in their hearts.* It was not God who tempted them. St. James specially warns us against such a doctrine, saying, "Let no man say when he is tempted, I am tempted of God." *God tempteth no man.* The very thought

is blasphemy, and the suggestion of Satan :
but God in His leadings heavenward, often
brings His people into very trying positions ;
and *Satan* taking advantage of these positions,
tempts us,—which God permits, *for the trial of
our faith.* If our faith fail not—if we trust
Him in the darkness, and when we know not
what He doeth,—great is the glory brought to
Him, and great the blessing to our own souls ;
for "Blessed is the man," says St. James,
"that endureth temptation : " and again :
"Count it all joy when ye fall into divers temptations." But if under trial *our faith fails,*
and instead of resting on God's Word we give
way to unbelief and murmuring,—great is
the triumph of the Tempter, great the dishonour to God, and great the damage to our
own souls.

It is quite true that it was God who had led
these children of Israel where they were. It
is quite true that it was because they had followed Him they had no bread and no water.
But it was not God who put the thought into
their hearts, " WE SHALL PERISH." SATAN,
taking advantage of the position into which
they had been led by the Spirit, *was its author ;*
and thereby, unwittingly to himself, worked out
God's purpose of proving both to Him and to

the Israelites, *what was in their hearts*. Was it
according to the profession they made when
they sang the song on the banks of the Red
Sea?

Oh, if instead of believing appearances, they
had believed the promise! If they had fed, not
on what they saw and felt, but on the Word
that had proceeded out of the mouth of God,—
that Word which had said, I will not only bring
you out, but *I will bring you in*,—how different
would have been the record left for our learning. How different is *the record left us by* THE
TRUE SEED OF ABRAHAM, when led by
God into the same position. (See the history,
in Matthew iv. 1.)

"Then was Jesus led up of the Spirit into
the wilderness, to be tempted of the devil.
And when He had fasted forty days and forty
nights, He was afterwards an hungered. And
when the Tempter came to Him, he said, If
Thou be the Son of God, command that these
stones be made bread. But He answered and
said, It is written, *Man shall not live by bread
alone, but by every word that proceedeth out of the
mouth of God.*"

Blessed Jesus! "In all points tempted like
as we are, yet without sin." "In that He
Himself hath suffered being tempted, He is

able also to succour them that are tempted."
(Hebrews ii. 18; iv. 15.) This He bore for
our sakes, leaving us an example *how we also
should contend with Satan.* Let us look for a
moment at the history, and may God the Holy
Spirit help us.

Immediately after His baptism at Jordan,
where He had received that glorious refreshing,
God the Spirit descending on Him in a bodily
shape, and the Father proclaiming audibly
from heaven, "This is my beloved Son, in
whom I am well pleased," was Jesus led into
the wilderness, as were the Israelites from Elim,
to be tempted of the devil. Forty days and
forty nights did His heavenly Father leave
Him without food,—His only companions the
wild beasts and Satan. Now, reader, I beseech
you remember this is a true history, and written
for our learning. How the holy human nature
of Jesus was supported for these forty days we
know not. God can support man without food,
though food cannot support man without God,
and He had for the same length of time before
supported both Moses and Elijah. (Deut. ix.
9; 1 Kings xix. 8.) But at the end of the
forty days it is recorded that Jesus "was an
hungered."

And now, taking advantage of His position,

comes the Tempter, and says, Make these stones bread : or, in other words, Give up Thy trust in God ; act for Thyself. Forty days hast Thou waited for Thy Father, and He has sent no deliverance ; now use the power which if Thou be the Son of God, Thou hast, and deliver Thyself. The end justifies the means : God cannot expect you to remain here and starve.

Such was one of the temptations to which our precious Saviour was exposed when following the leadings of the Spirit of God. Remember He did not *place Himself* in temptation,—that would have made all the difference ; but, while following the leadings of God's Spirit, He was tempted by the devil. Now how does He meet it ? As the Israelites did, by murmuring ; or as Satan suggested, by acting independently of His Father ? God forbid ; for then no flesh could have been saved : but He met it, not with these, but with "the *sword of the Spirit which is the Word of God*." Not for one moment did He consider His own position, or the means of deliverance which He held in His own power; but, looking away from SELF to those stores of Scripture which dwelt so richly in Him, He inquired, *What do they say* for the guidance of God's children in circumstances such as Mine ? and then answered the Tempter with—

"IT IS WRITTEN!"

It is written! Oh, the mighty power of these
words, if men would only believe *what is written!*
Jesus, in His life-long conflict with the devil,
had meat to eat which the world knew not of;
and this meat was "*every word that proceedeth
out of the mouth of God.*" It was the light to
His feet, and the lamp to His path. Long
before He appeared on our earth as the Son
of Man, did the Prophet Isaiah say of Him,
"He shall not judge after the sight of His eyes,
neither reprove after the hearing of His ears."
He judged nothing by appearance. He only
believed what His Father said. He only spoke
as His Father commanded. He only wished
what His Father willed. He only rejoiced at
what seemed good in His Father's sight, and
He only judged all these things according to
His Father's Word. *Therefore*, in the wilderness, in the beginning of His temptations did
He three times repel Satan: His only weapon
—"It is written!" "It is written!" "It is
written!" *Therefore* did He come victorious
out of every after-trouble and trial, and snare
of men and devils; *therefore* did He triumph
over sin, and death, and hell, and him who had
the power of death; *therefore* could He go down

into the grave and say, "On the third day I
shall rise again;" *therefore* does He now make
ceaseless intercession for His people,—certain,
because God has said so, that of those whom
His Father has given Him He shall lose none;
and *therefore*, though Satan still seems to reign
the God of this world, does He rest in certain
assurance on the yet unfulfilled promise: "I
shall give Thee the heathen for Thy inheritance,
and the uttermost parts of the earth for Thy
possession."

Oh, the almighty power of faith! "All
things are possible to him that believeth."
Of all that God has promised, not one good
thing ever has failed, or ever will fail, the Man
Christ Jesus. Of all that God has promised,
not one good thing ever has failed, or ever will
fail, the man who like Christ Jesus regardeth
not appearances, but puts his trust IN THE
WRITTEN WORD OF GOD.

Most earnestly would I recommend to every
one in times of ease and quiet, the diligent
study of the Word of God; and if you, oh
reader, have the care of children, teach them
to commit to memory large portions of Scripture. *It may come back to them with blessing
when you are in your grave.* As for yourself, not
only read it, but *meditate upon it, and habituate*

yourself to act upon it, and to rest upon it. Doing this in your every-day life, then the hour of your great trial, come when it may, will not take you unawares; but you will be able to resist the devil as Jesus resisted him, and to fight with the sword of the Spirit the good fight of faith.

Remember that we cannot meet Satan with what is written, unless we *know* what is written. Oh, if Jesus had not known the Scriptures when Satan assaulted Him, what would He have done? If you do not know them when he assaults you, what will you do? Also we may be certain of this,—that any unscriptural endeavour to escape from the position into which God brings us, will most surely make matters worse for us rather than better. Satan is ever ready to tempt us to this. To the Israelites he suggested—Return into Egypt; to Jesus—Make these stones bread; but let us be sure that it is far better for us to accept the apparently hard leadings of God—the stones of the wilderness—than to purchase a little present ease by taking the DEVIL's BREAD. Follow God's Spirit through life, and He may lead you to sow in tears; but in the end you shall most assuredly reap the finest of the wheat: but attend to Satan's teaching, and

follow him for the sake of the crumbs that fall
from his table, and no matter how great the
gratification now, you will find his bread turn
at last into a great millstone, that will sink you
soul and body into everlasting ruin.

And now, having considered the conduct of
these Israelites towards God, let us look a little
at His conduct towards them

Their sin was very great. Nothing less than
believing what they saw and felt, rather than
what God said. Nor was it committed for the
first time. In Egypt, at Pihahiroth, at Marah
had God brought these people into positions
of difficulty, and danger, and discomfort; and
that for the express purpose of proving what
was in their hearts. And in each of these
positions they had proved themselves without
faith,—without which it is "impossible to please
God." (Heb. xi. 6.) Still on each occasion,
having proved them, He forgave their sin without upbraiding, delivered them out of all their
troubles, and continued as their Leader His
guiding towards Canaan.

But what will He do now? Oh, what a
picture does the simple Bible record give us
of God's character: "Slow to anger and of
great goodness." The people said, "Ye have
brought us forth into the wilderness to kill this

whole assembly with hunger." And the Lord
said,—He who could have consumed them in a
moment said, "*Behold I will rain bread from
heaven for you, and the people shall go out and
gather a certain rate every day.*" The people
said, "Thou hast brought us up out of Egypt,
to kill us and our children and our cattle with
thirst."

And the Lord said, "*Behold I will stand
before thee upon the rock in Horeb, and, thou shalt
smite the rock, and there shall come water out of it,
that the people may drink.*"

What a contrast between man's treatment
of God, and God's treatment of man! and how
true the Scripture which says, My ways are
not as your ways. May the Holy Spirit teach
us never to judge God by our own standard;
never to argue,—*thus God will act*, because we
feel *that we would act so* if placed in His
position.

As I have already in this little book, in the
three chapters entitled "God's way of Salvation," endeavoured to give, as plainly and as
clearly as I could, an account of the scheme of
redemption, I do not intend in this place to
make more than one observation on each of
these two great types of Christ,—the Manna
and the Smitten Rock.

The children of Israel were perishing. They were in a waste wilderness where there was no food. No effort or energy of their own could avert a certain and speedy death. Every moment it was drawing nearer; and unless God works a miracle in their favour, their destruction is a certainty. But God will and does work a miracle in their favour,—for heaven and earth shall pass away, but His Word shall not pass away: and those cannot perish in the wilderness, of whom God has said, *I will bring you into the land of Canaan.*

It is true there was no bread in the wilderness; it is true that no effort of their own could procure it: but, to give the history in the language of the Psalmist,—God opened the doors of heaven, and rained down manna for them to eat, and gave them of the corn of heaven. "Man did eat angels' food: He sent them meat to the full." (See Ps. lxxviii. 25, etc.) *But with the food came the commandment for its gathering:* "The people shall go out, and gather a certain rate every day."

Observe: the manna was from God. His free and Sovereign gift to the people. Without it, they must every one, without exception, have perished. Yet was it not in the least degree procured by any work or effort of their own.

It came to them of His mercy, in their extremest
need; a daily monument before their eyes of
His power, and love, and truth.

But though the food was freely given them,
the Israelite would surely perish that neglected
the commandment for the gathering. It was
placed before all, without money and without
price; but it was *to be gathered*, and not only
gathered, but gathered *in the way of God's
appointment;* and he who attempted to gather
it in any other way, would as surely have found
that it would not sustain his life, as he who
refused to gather it at all. Some thought to
save themselves the trouble of a daily gathering, and to collect in one day what should
serve them for two or more. But so used, the
very bread of God became corrupted, for we
read, "*it bred worms and stank.*"

And thus it is with Christ, the "True Bread
from heaven." As the manna was the gift of
God to the Israelites, so is Christ the gift of
God to sinners,—free to *whosoever will;* and as
every Israelite in the camp was not only welcome, but commanded to gather what God had
provided for the salvation of his body, so is
every individual sinner that hears of Christ, not
only welcome, but commanded to accept what
God has provided for the salvation of his soul;

but though the gift is free, it must be gathered and gathered fresh every morning.

I am not now speaking of *making* a soul alive, but of *keeping* a soul alive. The soul who once by the power of the Holy Ghost feeds on Christ, is made alive from that moment, and shall most surely never perish. "I am the Living Bread," says Jesus (John vi. 51), "which came down from heaven: *if any man eat of this bread he shall live for ever.*" Therefore it is a statement as true as Christ Himself is true, that if a man really once eats of this Bread, he "HATH everlasting life," and shall never perish. But the proof that we have eaten is that we have spiritual life; and the proof that we have spiritual life, is that we seek spiritual food. Let no man think he can keep his soul alive by feeding on the experiences of days gone by. *The manna must be gathered fresh every morning.* The Bible must be read, and the teaching and guidance of the Holy Spirit daily sought by prayer, or he who once seemed to run well, will soon be a backslider; and unless he repents and does the first works, will end in being cast away.

I will here quote two of six short rules I some time since published for the guidance of young Christians: and may God the Spirit bless them.

Never neglect daily private prayer : and when you pray, remember that God is present, and that He hears your prayers.

Never neglect daily private Bible reading; and when you read, remember that God is speaking to you, and that you are to believe and act upon what He says.

I believe all blacksliding begins with the neglect of these two rules. Oh, then, *whether you feel appetite or not,* go to your Bible and your God in prayer, and seek fresh food for your soul every morning.

But God not only gave them bread to eat, but water to drink. The people said, "Thou hast brought us up out of Egypt to kill us, and our children and our cattle with thirst." And the Lord said, "Behold I will stand before thee there upon the rock in Horeb, and thou shalt smite the rock, and there shall come water out of it, that the people may drink."

Marvellous type of God's purpose in smiting Christ! The rock was smitten that water might flow forth; Christ was smitten that the Holy Ghost might flow forth.

Our precious Saviour has Himself explained to us that water, in Scripture, is the great type of the Holy Spirit. "He that believeth on Me," said Jesus, on the great day of the feast at

Jerusalem, "He that believeth on Me, out of his belly shall flow rivers of living water." And then we have the interpretation: "This spake He of the Spirit, which they that believe on Him should receive." Now man's curse, man's death, man's damnation, call it by what name you please, is simply this,—that by nature he is "WITHOUT GOD." All that we can imagine of evil is contained in these words: "WITHOUT God." It is SPIRITUAL DEATH;" it is the death that Adam died when he sinned in Paradise; it is the death that we have all died in Adam: as his seed every member of the human family is born into the world "WITHOUT GOD." It is the death that Christ died for us when He cried in agony, "My God, my God, why hast Thou forsaken Me!"

The great object of Christ in coming into the world, was not only to bring back man to God, but to bring back God to man. Had it not been that Christ was smitten, wounded for our transgressions, bruised for our iniquities, man never could have known God, except as a consuming fire. But THE ROCK WAS smitten,— Christ died; yea, rather is risen again; and now He has ascended up on high, and received gifts for men; yea, even for the rebellious, *that the Lord God might dwell among them*. (Ps. lxviii.

18.) And when, by the grace of God, we feel the motion of God in our own souls, or see the work of the Spirit of God shinning forth in the conduct of others, it becomes us to make melody to the Lord in our hearts, and to know of a surety, as Peter did at the day of Pentecost, that Jesus being by the right hand of God exalted, and having received of the Father the promise of the Holy Ghost, hath shed forth *this* which we now see and hear. Had the rock never been smitten there would have been no water in the wilderness, and every Israelite must have perished; had Christ never been smitten there would have been no gift of the Holy Ghost given, and every Child of Adam must have perished.

"Oh, that men would praise the Lord for His goodness, and for His wonderful works to the children of men!" GOD, NOW, THROUGH JESUS CHRIST, CAN AND WILL GIVE HIS HOLY SPIRIT TO THEM THAT ASK HIM.

XV.

The Christian Warfare.

" Then came Amalek and fought with Israel."

OH, the ups and downs of Christian life! God so orders it for the trial of our faith, and His teaching is, "Look not at the things which are seen, but at the things which are not seen."

The Israelites, a little while ago so despondent, have now got their bread and their water, and are once more confident and happy. Surely now, say they, our troubles are at an end, and we shall meet with no more hindrance on our road to Canaan. The want of bread and water was a dreadful trial, but it is past now, and we are safe. The Egyptians are all dead; there is no fear of our being again enslaved by them; food is provided for our journey; our bread shall be given us, and our water shall be sure; and there is nothing left for us to do, but to march leisurely on to the promised land.

But was this their experience? Was it ever the experience of any Christian? Let us look at the history written for our learning. The 6th and 7th verses of Exodus xvii. tell us of the gift of water; and the 8th, that no sooner was this boon granted, no sooner were they relieved from this fear, than "THEN CAME AMALEK AND FOUGHT WITH ISRAEL."

The Christian life may be compared to a ladder: no sooner is a man up one step than he sees another above him, and he must mount it, or he will never reach the top. His first step is off the earth, on the ladder—BOTH FEET; for the man who has one foot on the ladder and one on the earth, cannot be be said to be on the ladder at all. *Professing Christians, think of this.* Now this first step, *to get on the ladder,* is a hard step to many: I mention it by way of example; for I do not say by any means it is the first known and felt conflict with every saved soul. There are many, the children of pious parents, and others, educated under peculiarly favourable Christian circumstances, who cannot tell you when they first came out from the world, closed with Christ, and put both feet on the ladder. They were always, as far their knowledge serves them, living godly lives, and they cannot tell you (nor is it needful that they should be able to tell you) the precise time when they were converted; but for all this, there has been, I suspect, even in the life of the most unchequered Christian, a time when he has seen a step before him difficult and painful to the flesh to take, and as trying to his faith as was the "*no bread and no water*" to the Israeltes; a step that has taxed his Christianity to the utmost, and forced him in much conflict to think, "If this could be got over, then all after would be easy." But I would ask that Christian, if, after he has surmounted the step which looked so difficult, and *was* so painful,—if he has not found, as did these Israelites, that there was more conflict and more trial before him; that no sooner was the difficulty about the bread and water got over, than "*then came Amalek and fought with Israel*"?

A Christian never regrets that he took the uphill step; on the contrary, he knows and acknowledges that it has brought its own reward. Still, he is soon made to feel, even the best and holiest amongst us, that one difficulty surmounted, another will succeed it;

and that though there may be a succession of triumphs, yet that here it is conflict not victory.

But if this is a lesson to be learned by those who have sought God early, still more is it so with those who, like the writer of this little book, and the great bulk of these Israelites, start long after childhood on the Christian journey. A trial or temptation comes, and there is not that well-regulated mind and early instilled Christian principle that Christian education alone can give. In us, the tribulation that worketh patience, and the patience that worketh experience, has yet to do its work. And in us, as in these Israelites newly brought out of the land of Egypt, there is apt to be an impatience under every trial, and a feeling that if only *this one* could be surmounted, then all would be easy afterwards. But God would teach us that this is not our rest, and if we ever think we have attained rest here, as surely as we are God's people, so surely will God disappoint us.

Every Christian may settle it as a truth in his own mind, that his whole life will be a life of conflict. At one time his faith will be tried. No bread, no water: I shall starve in the wilderness. At another, under the influence of fightings within and fears without, he will be tempted

to cry, "All these things are against me."
And then the bread is given, and the water is
made sure; the fighting ceases, and the fears
with the fighting; so that the poor soldier of
Jesus having nothing more to desire, sits down
contented with the thought, "I am rich and
increased with goods, and have need of nothing." THEN COMES AMALEK, AND FIGHTS WITH
ISRAEL.

AMALEK! THE FLESH. These Israelites had
come out from Egypt. The Red Sea rolled
between them and the land of their captivity.
All necessary food was provided for their
journey. God gave them bread from heaven.
What could they want more? ONE THING:
*power against one enemy. Oh, God, give it me!
Oh, reader, pray for it for both of us!* Power
against an enemy who did not show himself
till the hour of ease and comfort—power against
Amalek, power against the flesh: then, when
every other enemy seemed subdued, "*then came
Amalek and fought with Israel.*"

Reader, have you come out from the world?
If so, bless God for it, for it was He who
brought you out. Now know, and never forget, that the same God who brought you out,
has provided for you, in His Word, all necessary provision for your heavenward journey.

Your food is, "*Every word that proceedeth out of the mouth of God.*" Feed on anything else, and it will poison you. But also know, and pray God that you may never forget it, that there is one foe who will walk side by side with you every step of your journey, whose sole object is to destroy you: AMALEK—THE FLESH. You may believe that you have escaped from Pharaoh; you may profess to be feeding on the bread that came down from heaven; but unless you are fighting against AMALEK,—aye not only fighting against, but overcoming THE FLESH, you will never enter into the heavenly Canaan.

I quote from Scripture the names of the powers this enemy brings against us: "Adultery, fornication, uncleanness, lasciviousness, idolatry, witchcraft, hatred, variance, emulations, wrath, strife, seditions, heresies, envyings, murders, drunkenness, revellings, *and such like:* of the which, says the Holy Ghost, "I tell you before, as I have also told you in time past, that they which do such things shall not inherit the kingdom of God." (Gal. v. 19—21.)

These are awful words; for, to drop the figure, the seeds of every one of these sins are in you, and in me, and in all. Some of them show more prominently in one person, some in another, as character, education, and other circumstances may call them into action; but no matter which of these sins it is that contends with us for the mastery, be it emulation or wrath, be it murder or adultery, as sure as God is the truth, we must get the victory over that sin, or perish; for thus saith the Lord, *" They which do such things shall not inherit the kingdom of God."* It is no sin to be tempted. The sin is *to be overcome by the temptation.* The commandment is, *" Resist the Devil:"* the promise is, *" He will flee from you.* The commandment is, *"Draw nigh to God:"* the promise is, *" He will draw nigh to you."* Jesus was tempted to worship the devil; but He said, " Get thee behind Me, Satan," and clung closely to His God. (James iv. 7, 8, and Luke iv. 8.)

Let us look, for a moment, at the Bible history of this transaction, that we may see how God taught Moses to contend with Amalek, and how Moses overcame him.

In the seventeenth chapter of Exodus we read, "Then came Amalek, and fought with Israel in Rephidim. And Moses said unto Joshua, Choose us out men, and go out, fight with Amalek: to-morrow I will stand on the

top of the hill with the rod of God in mine
hand. So Joshua did as Moses had said to
him, and fought with Amalek: and Moses,
Aaron, and Hur went up to the top of the hill.
And it came to pass when Moses held up
his hand, that Israel prevailed: and when he
let down his hand, Amalek prevailed. But
Moses' hands were heavy; and they took a
stone, and put it under him, and he sat thereon;
and Aaron and Hur stayed up his hands, the
one on the one side, and the other on the other
side; and his hands were steady until the going
down of the sun. And Joshua discomfited
Amalek and his people with the edge of the
sword.

"And the Lord said unto Moses, Write this
for a memorial in a book, and rehearse it in the
ears of of Joshua: for I will utterly put out the
remembrance of Amalek from under heaven.
And Moses built an altar, and called the name
of it JEHOVAH-nissi: for He said, Because the
Lord hath sworn that the Lord will have
war with Amalek from generation to generation."

Now we are here taught how Moses met
and overcame this enemy, who stood between
him and the land of Canaan. He bade Joshua
choose out men, and fight against Amalek;

while he, Moses himself, with Aaron, and Hur, went to the top of the hill, with the rod of God in his hand; or, in other words, while he used every means in his own power against Amalek, he looked to God, and God alone, for the victory. To have fought in his own strength against Amalek would have been utterly unavailing; for when Moses let down his hands, no matter how great the efforts of Joshua, Amalek invariably prevailed. Still, had Joshua not done his utmost against him, the prayers of Moses would have been unavailing also, because the means would not have been used that God had put in his power. In all our conflicts we must both PRAY AND STRIVE. The two cannot be separated. It is God that giveth the victory. But as the farmer plants his land, though he cannot make the crops grow, so the sinner must work out his own salvation, as if it all depended on himself; still after every separate triumph, let him give God the glory. God records that "Joshua discomfited Amalek," and God is often pleased to speak this way of His people; but I am quite sure that Joshua said it was God that had discomfited him. (Exodus xvii. 13.)

And never think, dear reader, that because THE FLESH fights against you it is useless to

continue your journey heavenward. To make
you so think is one of Satan's great desires.
First, he will inject evil into you, and then
prompt the thought that because of this evil
you are too bad to be saved. But believe him
not. The blood of Jesus Christ, God's Son,
cleanses from all sin; and it was because you
are bad, worse even than Satan or your own
heart can paint you, that God made a way
through His own beloved Son, by which He
might forgive your sins, and come and help
you against all your enemies. Fight on, and
strive on; and your victory is certain, if you
look, not to your fighting and striving, *but to
Jesus*. Remember that when you are fighting
against your corruptions, you are fighting not
only against your own enemies but *against
God's enemies:* and that He is even more in-
terested in your victory than you are yourself.
He is the COMMANDER, you are the fighting
soldier: only follow your Leader, and who is
he that shall harm you? Has God not sworn
that He will have war with Amalek from
generation to generation? Has he not said
that He will put out the remembrance of
Amalek from under heaven? As a good
soldier of Jesus Christ, endure hardness now,
and you shall surely be made more than

conqueror through Him who loved you. The conflict will often be severe; sometimes even (which may God forbid) Amalek may get a victory, and then Satan will surely tempt you with the thought that you are lost for ever: but heed him not. Most true it is written, "Sin not:" most true it is written, "The soul that sinneth it shall die;" but it is also written, "*If any man sin we have an Advocate with the Father, Jesus Christ the Righteous: and He is the propitiation for our sins.* (1 John ii. 2.) The devil will induce you to sin if he can, that *through your sin* he may tempt you to unbelief. He tempted Peter and Judas both to sin, and to both doubtless he whispered the same lie: Your sin is too great to be forgiven. Judas believed him, but Peter did not; so Judas, in his unbelief of Christ, who had said "Him that cometh to Me I will in no wise cast out," went away and hanged himself; while Peter went back to Jesus and was forgiven. All Scripture bears me out in saying, had Judas gone to Jesus he would have been forgiven also. Oh, can you imagine Judas at the feet of Jesus, saying, "Do forgive me!" and Jesus saying, "No: I will not!"

Never, dear reader, give up hope; never give up faith in Jesus because the "*the flesh*" fights against you. "The flesh lusteth against the Spirit, and the Spirit against the flesh;" and if there was no conflict in us there would be no sign of the Holy Spirit's presence. We must expect Amalek to fight with Israel, but Israel must also be prepared to fight with Amalek, in the sure and certain hope that he will be more than conqueror.

XVI.

The Fleshpots.

THIS little book has already extended to a far greater length than I originally intended; and were I to touch on every sin wherewith these Israelites provoked God in the wilderness, I should only repeat what I have already written, and perhaps weaken it. I pass over, therefore, the idolatry of the golden calf, and the many other provocations whereby they at length so angered God, "that had not Moses, His chosen "—type of that CHOSEN ONE who ever liveth to make intercession for His people,—" had not Moses, His chosen, stood before Him in the breach to turn away His wrath," He would have destroyed the whole multitude together, and made of him a nation greater and mightier than they. I will leave these things, however, to the prayerful and diligent consideration of the reader, and take up the history again in the eleventh of Numbers.

There we read of the sin which immediately preceded the unbelief for which God sware in His wrath that this generation should never enter into the land of Canaan.

Before I advert, however, to this sin, *which is so often the forerunner of final apostasy*, I would ask your attention to the confession of David in the 106th Psalm.

In that Psalm, where he recites at length the sins of these Israelites, David opens the history with these remarkable words: " *We have sinned with our fathers, we have committed iniquity, we have done wickedly;* " and then proceeds with the record, *not of what he*, but of what these Israelites, *his fathers* had done. David thus says what St. Paul said afterwards, in Romans iii. 9, where he asks the question, " Are we," —that is I, the Apostles, and you sinners of the Gentiles, who have been converted to Christianity,—"Are we better than they," the people, " whose damnation is just?" and then replies (yet not he but the Holy Ghost), " *No: in no wise.*" Thus David's object, and Paul's object, and, I would reverently add, my object, is to show that the best of us are no better than the chief of sinners; so far from it, that as face answereth to face in water, so our hearts are not only precisely similar to those of these

Israelites, but to the hearts of all sinners in all generations, and produce precisely the same fruits. Did they commit iniquity? So do we. Did they fail to understand God's wonders? So do we. Did they provoke Him? So do we. Did they forget His works, and act without His counsel? So do we. Did they lust after evil things? So do we. Did they tempt God? So do we. Did they make idols? So do we. In which one of their sins are we not obliged to say with David, "*We have sinned with our fathers*"? In which part of their conduct towards God "*are we better than they*"? The conduct of these Israelites has been recorded for our learning; and they are "OURSELVES : A PICTURE."

In the eleventh chapter of the Book of Numbers, and at the 4th verse we read : "And the mixed multitude that was among them fell a lusting : and the children of Israel also wept again and said, Who shall give us flesh to eat? We remember the fish which we did eat in Egypt freely; the cucumbers, and the melons, and the leeks, and the onions, and the garlick. But now our soul is dried away : there is nothing at all beside this manna before our eyes."

Oh, it is a bad, bad sign of a man when, after having made a profession of Christianity, after having gone a certain length, and remained apparently steadfast a certain time, he begins to look back to the fleshpots of Egypt. Beware of it, beware of it, as you would not lose your soul. Reject and resist the first such thought, as you would reject poison, or resist the murderer. What! after they had gone so far, overcome so many difficulties, and escaped so many dangers,—now that their salvation is apparently so much nearer than when they believed, are the hearts of these Israelites to be drawn away from God by "the leeks, and the onions, the garlick, and the other things" of Egypt? Alas, yes! for the Bible records it. And what multitudes who once seemed to be of the number of God's people are now amongst the lost,—whose first backsliding commenced in a longing desire for something, not unlawful in itself, but *for something that was not Christ!* Oh, professing Christian, beware of the first thought, *" Nothing but this manna!"* When it is put into the language of the present day it takes some such form as this: I cannot be always thinking about Jesus: I cannot be always speaking or working for Him; I am sure God does not want us to make ourselves miserable, and something besides religion is absolutely necessary.

Now I would earnestly ask any who have thoughts and feelings such as these, what spirit in you do you think it is that prompts them? *Do you believe it is the Holy Spirit?* Do you think it is the Holy Spirit that ever puts the idea into any man's head that it is, and would be a miserable life to be always thinking about Christ, to be always speaking or working for Jesus? *You know it is not.* And if it is not the Holy Spirit, then it is *the unholy spirit,* the Spirit of Evil, the Father of Lies, who wishes to cheat you out of true happiness both here and hereafter.

Let me ask you solemnly and prayerfully to consider this question. Do you not believe that there is sufficient in Christ *to satisfy* the soul that really makes Him HIS ALL. *You know you do:* you dare not say you do not. Then if you do not find in Him a satisfying portion, is it not precisely for this very reason, that you are trying to seek it *partly* in Him and partly in something else? Your belief is (for *our faith is shown by our works*) that to have A LITTLE OF CHRIST AND A LITTLE OF THE WORLD WILL MAKE YOU HAPPIER THAN TO HAVE A GREAT DEAL OF CHRIST AND NOTHING OF THE WORLD! Oh, away with such a doctrine, begotten by the devil, in the lusts and lies of your own heart. There is no satisfying portion out of Christ; and the most truly happy man is he who knows most of Jesus. Oh, if you and I could only see the beauty of the Lord, as I feel quite sure it may be seen even on this earth,— if you and I were walking in the light (see 1 John i. 7), as we might walk, and had felt fellowship and communion with the Father and His Son Jesus Christ, as we might have,—no leek, or melon, or onion, or other thing of the fleshpots of Egypt could weigh with us for one moment in comparison with "THE LIVING BREAD WHICH CAME DOWN FROM HEAVEN." (John vi. 51.)

It is because we do *not* walk in the light that we do not see the beauty of the Lord; and it is because we do not see the beauty of the Lord that we cry, "*Nothing but this manna!*" and desire the stimulating influences of the fleshpots of Egypt. Let us pray, as David did (Psalm xxvii. 4), that we may behold the beauty of the Lord.

Reader, does it so happen that you are amongst the number of those who once sought Christ and found Him precious? Can you remember a time when you found your happiness in reading His Word and doing His work? And do you know that the love of other things has crept in, and so blinded you that you cannot now see Jesus as you used to see Him; that your heart has turned aside after the leeks, and onions, and garlic of Egypt, and that He is no longer to you the chiefest among ten thousand, altogether lovely?

Do you know, too, that you are trying to convince yourself and others that you are not really a backslider; but that man needs some pleasure, some relaxation, beyond the pleasure of doing everything to the glory of God, and doing nothing that he cannot do in the name of Jesus. *If so, be sure you have not a moment to lose in throwing yourself at the feet of God, and beseeching Him to show you more of Christ.* Oh, it is an awful time with any such soul, for either *Christ will grow more precious or less precious.* Amalek, of whom we spoke in the last chapter, seemed to be discomfited; but this state of heart is Amalek come again: Amalek in another and more dangerous shape; Amalek the flesh, lusting against God the Spirit.

I would wish to speak very strongly, and very plainly on this subject; for I believe getting the victory in this battle to be the distinguishing mark, and the turning point between the true child of God and the self-deceiver. A man hears the Gospel, and he cries, "The blood of Jesus Christ, God's Son,

cleanseth us from all sin ; " and in the reception
of this truth, finds joy and peace. He next
makes a profession, and comes out from the
world, as these Israelites came out of Egypt.
Then, probably, very soon after, comes Amalek,
in the shape of some strong trial or temptation,
and fights with Israel. He comes openly, he
comes boldly, as he did upon the Israelites in
the wilderness; there is no room for temporiz-
ing, no hope of quarter: it is " *Overcome me,
or perish !* " and the young professor, frightened
and dismayed, calls upon the Name of the Lord,
fights that particular battle, overcomes that particular temptation, and discomfits Amalek. And
then he is certain that he is a Christian, and
has great peace and great confidence: confidence
that perhaps soon becomes vain confidence ; and
the soldier of the cross is tempted to put off
his armour, to lie down in sloth, and feed on
Scriptures that speak of the gift of Christ, to
the neglect of those that call to prayerfulness,
and watchfulness, and self-denial. He believes,
he says, *that Christ died for him*, and therefore,
of necessity, everything must be well with him.

But soon, stealthily, and imperceptibly, and
when least expected, back comes Amalek. Not
now as an open foe to fight with Israel, but to
suggest to the professor that God does not

require such a very strict Christianity; and
how pleasurable, or how profitable it would be
to return in some slight degree to the world.
In ways as various as are the carnal tastes and
dispositions of men, he suggests what he suggested to the Israelites: "Who shall give us
flesh to eat? there is nothing at all beside this
manna before our eyes."

Now it is this time of trial, a time that I
believe not only every child of God must pass
through, but against which he must be continually on the watch, that tests, the faith of us
all, of what sort it is. If it is the faith which
justifieth, and which is the work of the Holy
Ghost in the heart, if it is the faith which is
the gift of God, and which St. Paul calls (Titus
i. 1), "the faith of God's elect," it will enable
the believer resolutely to refuse, let his hunger-
ings and thirstings be what they may, to seek
to satisfy them with anything but "*manna*."
By this faith he knows (not FEELS, observe, but
KNOWS), that Christ is the True Bread that came
down from heaven! that however distasteful
He may be to the natural man, to feed on
anything else is to feed on ashes: and in spite
of Amalek and all his army, he clings to Him
as his only satisfying portion. But if the faith
of the professor be the faith of those described

in Luke viii. 13, who when they hear, receive the Word with joy, but have no root: who for a while believe, but in time of tempation fall away; then, sooner or later, no matter what his doctrines, or frames, or experiences may have been, he will surely weep again after the things of Egypt; and the same cry that went up from these Israelites will go up from him: "Who shall give us flesh to eat? We remember the fish which we did eat in Egypt freely, the cucumbers, and the melons, and the leeks, and the onions, and the garlic. But now our soul is dried away: there is nothing at all beside this manna before our eyes."

The same Bible which says, "Believe on the Lord Jesus Cnrist, and thou shalt be saved," says also, "If ye live after the flesh, ye shall die;" and the evidence not only to others, that we are true Christians, but also to ourselves, is, that when the flesh lusteth against the Spirit, and the Spirit against the flesh, we are led by the Spirit, and crucify the flesh.

Paul said, Christ "loved me, and gave Himself for me;" but he also says, in the same verse, "I am crucified with Christ;" and no man has any scriptural warrant for saying Christ was crucified for me, who does not know, however much the flesh may harass, and tempt, and *even on an occasion overcome*, that he is habitually crucifying himself for Jesus.

Oh, I would beseech you, watch against, and however painful it may be, *deny* the first felt cravings after *the old fleshpots*. They will eat as doth a canker, and will increase unto more ungodliness. The thing desired may be lawful, or unlawful in itself, I believe *that* makes little difference; for if it is something that God has seen fit to deny us, it is unlawful to lust and crave after it. There was no sin in these Israelites eating flesh: "every gift of God is good, and to be received with thankfulness;" their sin was to desire a thing unto murmuring and repining, which God had not seen fit to give them.

It is a solemn word that the Holy Ghost speaks by the mouth of St. Paul, when rightly interpreted: "Let your conversation be without covetousness, and be content with such things as ye have." "They that WILL BE RICH,"—and I take this to allude not to the love of money only, but to the coveting and unlawful striving after anything that God has not seen fit to grant us,—"THEY THAT WILL BE RICH fall into temptation, and a snare, and into many foolish and hurtful lusts, which drown men in destruction and perdition." Oh,

how many have proved in their own experience
the truth of these Scriptures! How many are
there who once thought themselves Christians,
but who now know in their hearts that they
have gone far away from God, who can remember the time when a first longing entered
into them for something He had not been
pleased to give them. It was not wicked
perhaps; still their conscience was not quite at
ease about it: for all that, however, they did
all they could to get it. The pursuit of it
occupied their minds, employed their time, and
took possession of that place in their hearts
that once seemed securely to belong to Christ;
at last, after much effort and energy,—*at last
they got what they wanted;* but they have never
been the same Christians since. What happened
to these Israelites happened to them. *" God
gave them their request; but sent leanness into their
soul."* (Ps. cvi. 15.)

XVII.

Unbelief.

THE last words of the last chapter were very fearful: "God gave them their request; but sent leanness into their soul." Yet even such should not despair, for to be lean is not to be dead; and, blessed be God, let him but diligently seek it, and the *lean soul may be made fat again.* (Prov. xiii. 4.)

The souls of these Israelites were in an unhealthy state; but for all that, God had not given them up. He still led them, and they still followed; and while this is the case, let the past have been what it may, we have the great Scriptural evidence that God has not cast us off; for, "as many as are led by the Spirit of God, they are the sons of God." (Rom. viii. 14.) Still their state was a state most favourable for the assaults of Satan, and one which too often ends in hardness and unbelief. *If you are in it, give God no rest till you are out of it.*

It was in this state of heart and mind, that the Israelites arrived at the borders of the promised land, from whence Moses, by the command of God, sent twelve men to examine the country and bring back a report of what sort it was. Let us, before we make any comment, take the history in the words of scripture.

In the thirteenth of Numbers we read: "And the Lord spake unto Moses, saying, Send thou men, that they may search the land of Canaan, which I give unto the children of Israel: of every tribe of their fathers shall ye send a man, every one a ruler among them. And Moses by the commandment of the Lord sent them from the wilderness of Paran: all those men were heads of the children of Israel.

"And Moses sent them to spy out the land of Canaan, and said unto them, Get you up this way southward, and go up into the mountain: and see the land, what it is; and the people that dwelleth therein, whether they be strong or weak, few or many; and what the land is that they dwell in, whether it be good or bad; and what cities they be that they dwell in, whether in tents, or in strongholds; and what the land is, whether it be be fat or lean, whether there be wood therein or not. And be ye of good courage, and bring of the fruit of the land.

"Now the time was the time of the first ripe grapes. So they went up, and searched the land from the wilderness of Zin unto Rehob, as men come to Hamath. And they ascended by the south, and came unto Hebron; where Ahiman, Sheshai, and Talmai, the children of Anak, were. And they came unto the brook of Eschol, and cut down from thence a branch with one cluster of grapes, and they bare it between two upon a staff; and they brought of the pomegranates and of the figs. The place was called the brook Eschol, because of the cluster of grapes which the children of Israel cut down from thence.

"And they returned from searching of the land after forty days. And they went and came to Moses, and to Aaron, and to all the congregation of the children of Israel, unto the wilderness of Paran, to Kadesh; and brought back word unto them, and unto all the congregation, and shewed them the fruit of the land. And they told him, and said, We came unto the land whither thou sentest us, and surely it floweth with milk and honey; and this is the fruit of it. Nevertheless the people be strong that dwell in the land, and the cities are walled, and very great: and moreover we saw the children of Anak there. The Amalekites dwell in the land of the south: and the Hittites, and the Jebusites, and the Amorites, dwell in the mountains: and the Canaanites dwell by the sea, and by the coast of Jordan.

"And Caleb stilled the people before Moses, and said, Let us go up at once, and possess it; for we are well able to overcome it. But the men that went up with him, said, We be not able to go up against the people; for they are stronger than we. And they brought up an evil report of the land which they had searched, unto the children of Israel, saying, The land through which we have gone to search it, is a land that eateth up the inhabitants thereof; and all the people that we saw in it are men of a great stature. And there we saw the giants, the sons of Anak, which come of the giants: and we were in our own sight as grasshoppers, and so we were in their sight.

"And all the congregation lifted up their voice, and cried; and the people wept that night. And all the children of Israel murmured against Moses and against Aaron: and the whole congregation said unto them, Would God that we had died in the land of Egypt! or would God that we had died in the wilderness! And wherefore hath the Lord brought us unto this land to fall by the sword, that our wives and our children should be a prey? were it not better for us to return into Egypt? And they said one to another, Let us make a captain, and let us return into Egypt.

"Then Moses and Aaron fell on their faces before all the assembly of the congregation of the children of Israel. And Joshua the son of Nun, and Caleb the son of Jephunneh, which were of them that searched the land, rent their clothes: and they spake unto all the company of the children of Israel, saying, The land, which we passed through to search it, is an exceeding good land. If the Lord delight in us, then He will bring us into this land, and give it us; a land which floweth with milk and honey. Only rebel not ye against the Lord, neither fear ye the people of the land; for they are bread for us: their defence is departed from them, and the Lord is with us: fear them not. But all the congregation bade stone them with stones.

"And the glory of the Lord appeared in the tabernacle of the congregation before all the children of Israel. And the Lord said unto Moses, How long will this people provoke Me? and how long will it be *ere they believe*

Me? As truly as I live, saith the Lord, as ye have spoken in mine ears, so will I do to you: your carcases shall fall in this wilderness; and all that were numbered of you according to your whole number, from twenty years old and upward, which have murmured against Me, doubtless ye shall not come into the land, concerning which I sware to make you dwell therein, save Caleb the son of Jephunneh, and Joshua the Son of Nun. After the number of the days in which ye searched the land, even forty days, each day for a year, shall ye bear your iniquities, even forty years, and ye shall know *my breach of promise.*"

Alas! alas for this great multitude! At last they have succeeded in bringing destruction on themselves. Oh, how often had they provoked God! How often had He forgiven them. He had rebuked, and He had chastened them; but it was as a father chasteneth his children; but never had one word ever come from His lips, but words to assure and strengthen. But "THEY BELIEVED NOT HIS WORD." And now He has sworn in His wrath, that they shall never enter into His rest. *Reader, take care.* "He that being often reproved hardeneth his neck, shall suddenly be destroyed, and that without remedy." (Prov. xxix. 1.)

The Scripture record that I have quoted, is
so plain and simple, that there is little room
or need for comment. It tells its own story,
so that he who runs may read.

Moses, by the command of God, sends out
spies, twelve men, a man from every tribe, to
spy out Canaan. After an absence of forty
days, they return and tell him and the congregation : " We came unto the land whither thou
sentest us, and surely it floweth with milk and
honey." They bring too of the fruit of the
land, in proof of what they said.

Now all this was very well, so far as it went;
but it never could end well, if it went no
further. To acknowledge that it is a good
land, will never bring any one into the land of
promise. Many, and many have gone thus
far, and further, who have never entered into
the kingdom. To talk about the excellencies
and desirableness of heaven, while we make
no effort to attain to it, is but another form of
the cry of Balaam : " Let me die the death of
the righteous, and let my last end be like his."
The joy, and the peace, and the rest of heaven
are good things no doubt : but before you can
enjoy them, oh professsor, you must overcome
Ahiman, Sheshai, Talmai, and the sons of Anak.

Many can talk fluently of the excellency of

the promised land who have no faith, and so
have no will, to go to war with the giants.
Yet must there be not only war, but victory,
before a man can enter into the rest of Canaan.
If God has chosen us at all, *He has chosen us to
be soldiers;* and as these spies well knew that if
ever they got possession of the land it must be
by conquest, so does every professor know that
if he is to enter into rest, he must not only
wish but *strive;* that the kingdom of Heaven
suffereth violence, and it is the violent who
take it by force; yet how many while they cry,
It is a good land, and a pleasant, have no more
heart to enter into conflict with their sins than
these spies had to enter into conflict with the
Canaanite, and the Hivite, and the Perizzite,
and the Jebusite.

"The land is a good land," said the spies,
"*nevertheless*" *(oh, beware of "nevertheless,"
where God has spoken plainly!)* "nevertheless
the people be strong that dwell in the land,
and the cities are walled, and very great: and
moreover we saw the children of Anak there,"
and we were no bigger than grasshoppers in
their sight.

Great is the influence for good or evil that
man possesses over his fellow-men, especially
when position, talent, wealth, or other extra-

neous circumstances place him in a rank somewhat above his fellows. The false teaching
and preaching of these ten spies, *all of them
heads of the children of Israel*, so affected the
hearts of the people that SIX HUNDRED THOUSAND
MEN, and probably somewhere about the same
number of women, believing it, *believed a lie;
and so turned God to be their enemy, and perished
in the wilderness!*

I hardly like to write all the solemn thoughts
to which this part of the history gives rise.
How often do we hear people say to those who
hold the doctrines contained in this little book
—"*If the religion that you teach is true, how very
few there are that will be saved.*" We scarcely
know how to reply to such; for judging the
world by the Bible, what they say IS SO VERY
TRUE. Known unto God are all His works,
and He has revealed to us, "that in all things
Christ shall have the pre-eminence." (Col. i.
18.) Therefore we would believe that God will
so arrange that the devil shall not have the
pre-eminence in the number of his people. But
this is almost trenching on the secret things of
God; and if it were not for the text I have
quoted, would seem an approach to seeking to
be wise above what is written. But it is not
being wise above what is written to say that

"strait is the gate, and narrow is the way which leadeth unto life, and few there be that find it." It is not being wise above what is written to say, that when in a company of six hundred thousand, there were only two men, Caleb and Joshua, who believed God's Word, God only saved those two men, and without a moment's hesitation, doomed all the rest to perish in the wilderness. It is not being wise above what is written to say, that while the most successful sermon ever preached on earth, a sermon preached under the direct teaching of the Holy Ghost, effectually worked faith to the salvation of only three thousand persons, this preaching in the wilderness, under the direct teaching of the devil, effectually worked unbelief to the destruction of about a million!

I will not pursue this subject. But *let him that is wise consider these things:* for truly as yet we do not see all things put under Christ; truly as yet Satan is the god of this world.

LORD JESUS, COME QUICKLY.

Of what consequence it is to whose teaching we listen. Let no man, for the sake of denominational difference, lose the vital ministry of a man of God. Many false prophets and false teachers are gone out into the world; and speaking in all charity, I cannot but believe that "MANY" is the word to be used as regards those that are being led by their teachers to Hell; and "FEW" as regards those that are being led to Heaveu. This I believe to be the fact throughout Christendom.

And how awful is the guilt of the false teacher, and how awful will be his doom at the day of judgment! These Israelitish false teachers were doubtless more guilty in the sight of God, than those who believed them, and God seems so to have meant us to understand the history; for it is recorded (Num. xiv. 37) "that those men that did bring up the evil report upon the land, died by the plague before the Lord;" yet, though immediate judgment was executed upon them, *it did not save from judgment the congregation that believed them*. Their carcases fell in the wilderness, BECAUSE THEY WERE TAUGHT ERROR AND BELIEVED IT.

Some might have judged that the Israelites were bound to believe these men, because they had been ordained by God and by Moses, and sent into Canaan for the express purpose of gathering information, and so fitting themselves to come back as instructors of the people; but this was not the judgment of God. HE did not see that the teacher, having been so ordained, was any excuse for the congregation, when they believed teaching that was contrary to His Word. Each member of the congregation of Israel knew, or if he did not, had no excuse for not knowing, that God had said, "*I will bring you into the land of Canaan;*" and when God's Word said one thing, and God's teacher another, THEY WERE BOUND TO BELIEVE GOD, RATHER THAN HIS TEACHER.

It is a great truth, though a truth hated and denied by multitudes both of teachers and congregations in the present day, *that every member of a congregation is bound to prove for himself, from the Word of God, that the doctrine of the man who teaches him is according to that Word.*

"To the law and to the testimony," says Isaiah to the Jews. "If they" (that is those who teach you) "speak not according *to this word, it is because there is no light in them.*" (Isaiah viii. 26.)

"Though we, or an angel from heaven," cries Paul, "preach any other Gospel, unto you, than that we have preached unto you, let him be accursed." (Gal. i. 8.)

"Thou has tried them which say they are Apostles, and are not, and hast found them liars," is the eulogizing address of the Saviour to the Church at Ephesus; and the same Spirit who spoke by the mouth of Isaiah, and Paul, and Jesus Himself, bears (Acts xvii. 11) this remarkable testimony to the congregations of Berea: that they were *more noble* than those of Thessalonica, in that they searched the Scriptures daily, to see whether the things spoken by Paul "*were so:*" and then adds, "THEREFORE *many of them believed.*" Thus in the Old Testament, and the New, as also in the book of Revelation, we have it plainly laid down, that the doctrines of the teacher, even though that teacher be an angel from heaven, are to be compared by his hearers with the teaching of the Word of God; and if they do not agree, *the doctrine of the teacher is to be rejected.*

ONE GUIDE has been given, and one only, by God to man: the written Word of God. And every human being who has a copy of the Bible, and can read it, is bound to search out in it, for himself, GOD'S WAY OF SALVATION.

The Holy Spirit is promised to all who ask Him; and those who seek Him need not that any man teach them, for they "*have an unction from the Holy One.*" (1 John ii. 20, 21.)

Let no one for a moment suppose that in making these remarks, I in the least intend to teach that a stated ministry is unnecessary.

God forbid. So far from it, I believe that a stated ministry in the Church is as much appointed by God, as I believe that the spies were appointed to spy out the land of Canaan. I believe that next to His word and His Spirit, a minister taught by the Holy Ghost is the best gift God has to give us; and such a minister will always desire that his people should judge his teaching by their Bibles: but what I do contend for is, that it will be no excuse for a man to say, if he is found to be a self-deceiver at the day of judgment, that he got his religion either *from his Church, or from his minister*.

There never was a time in the Church when there were not false prophets and false teachers. 2 Peter ii. 1, puts this truth very briefly, but very strongly: "There were false prophets also among the people, even as *there shall be* false teachers among you, who privily shall bring in *damnable heresies*:" and I believe that as faith in the word of these spies was the destruction of the Israelites, so faith in the word of teachers who bring in "*damnable heresies*" has been and will be the everlasting destruction of millions upon millions. On the other hand, I believe that there will not be found a lost one at the last day who can honestly plead with God, "I got my religion from the Bible, which I studied in the name of Jesus Christ, with earnest prayer for the teaching of the Holy Spirit." Such students of theology may not see "eye to eye" in all matters at present; but they shall all see enough to make Jesus their Alpha and Omega, their beginning and their ending. Of God He shall be made unto them "Wisdom, and Righteousness, and Sanctification, and Redemption," and every one of them shall appear before God in Zion.

An now, let us inquire what was the particular sin for which God destroyed these teachers, and doomed those who believed them to perish in the wilderness. St. Paul asks the same question, and answers it in Heb. iii. 18: "To whom sware He that they should not enter into His rest, but to them that believed not." So we see that they could not enter in *because of unbelief.*

UNBELIEF! Dear reader, this was the sin for which God excluded Israel from Canaan; and UNBELIEF *is the sin for which every hearer of the Gospel who perishes, will perish at the last day.* THERE IS NO OTHER SIN DAMNING TO a Gospel HEARER, BUT UNBELIEF. Oh, I beseech you to beware of rejecting what I say, until you have searched your Bible, with prayer, to see if it is the Word of God: for if I am right, and you

believe me not, what must be your future?
You will be yourself an eternal illustration of
my doctrine, and perish "BECAUSE OF UNBELIEF."

There are ten commandments under the law;
and a man may have broken over and over
again, every one of these, and yet be saved:
for if he repents, and goes to God by Jesus
Christ, God can, and for Christ's sake, will
forgive him. *Christ casts out none, and His
Blood cleanses from all sin.* But let any man on
any excuse whatever, break *the one commandment under the Gospel*,—to believe in the name
of the Lord Jesus Christ; let him appear before
God, with any plea, but *His atonement, His
Blood,* and—no matter how conscientiously he
may have followed the teaching of his Church,
his minister, or his own conscience,—he will
perish, as these Israelites did; not for any
particular sin that he has committed, but " *because of unbelief.*"

A child of God, and a believer in Jesus, are
but different names for the same thing; for it
is by faith, and faith only, that we are made
the children of God: " We are all the children
of God by faith in Christ Jesus " (Gal. iii. 26);
and the fearful and unbelieving professor will
be as surely excluded from heaven, as will the
murderer and adulterer.

Does this offend you? I cannot retract it; for God has declared the same in His written Word. (Rev. xxi. 8.)

Some will tell you now-a-days, that if a man is sincere, and really believes what he professes, for an error in doctrine, or as they prefer to term it, an error in judgment, God will not condemn him. But I would ask such, Is it so written in the Bible? Is that what we are taught, say in the first four verses of the tenth chapter to the Romans? My own creed is, that so far from the belief of error being a palliation of man's sin, it is the teaching of the Bible, from Genesis to Revelation, that there is nothing more opposed to God, or more thoroughly abominable in His sight, than THE SINCERE BELIEF OF THE NATURAL HEART OF MAN.

There could not be more sincere or genuine faith than was the faith of these Iraelites, both teachers and hearers. They said, "It is impossible for us to get into Canaan:" *and they thoroughly believed it.* It was the true and heartfelt faith of their inmost souls; and there was not a particle of hypocrisy in that vast multitude. It is true that they could quite easily have got into the land of Canaan, for God had said He would bring them in; but for all that they were most sincerely convinced that it was an utter impossibility. Did their sincerity save them. Did God consider it an excuse for their unbelief? So far from an excuse, it was their very faith that was their sin; and *the sin* for which they perished in the wilderness: for in holding this faith THEY MADE GOD A LIAR.

How often have I said in this little book that our senses, our reason, and our feelings are false and lying guides; and never to be believed when they contradict the Word of God. Whenever I have said this, I have spoken the truth as it is in Jesus; and whenever I have said this, I have spoken that truth, which of all others the natural heart of man can neither receive nor believe. These Israelites are "OURSELVES: A PICTURE."

Six hundred thousand men came out of Egypt by Moses. Of this vast multitude, two, and two only, Caleb the son of Jephunneh, and Joshua the son of Nun, entered the promised land. Why? Again we answer, in the words of the Holy Spirit, "*because of unbelief;*" because, among these six hundred thousand men, Caleb the son of Jephunneh, and Joshua the son of Nun, were the only two that believed God's word: they believed what He said, and received the promises; the rest believed what they saw and felt, and perished in the wilderness

And oh, how beyond all praise was the faith of these two men, and how precious was the fruit that it produced! What glory it brought to God; what blessing on themselves. Hath the Scripture said in vain, "Whosoever believeth on Him shall not be ashamed." At the risk of their lives did Caleb and Joshua stand up in the face of the whole assembled multitude of unbelievers, and preach SALVATION BY FAITH.

Everything was against these two lone and solitary men, except the Word of God; but, like Jesus in the wilderness, they fed and acted on that. Their's was a glorious cry: "Let us go up at once, and possess the land, for we are well able to overcome it." They are mighty; we are weak. They are giants; we are grasshoppers. But it is neither might nor power in this battle: the question is, on which side is the Lord? "*Their defence has departed from them, and the Lord is with us.*" (Num. xiv. 9.) And how did the people listen to this teaching? "*All the congregation bade stone them with stones.*" (Num. xiv. 10.)

From that day to this, the great mass of mankind have received the same teaching in the same spirit.

But there was another Listener besides the

people, and how did He listen to this teaching? Read Num. xiv. 10—38. I quote a portion: "And the glory of the Lord appeared in the tabernacle of the congregation before all the children of Israel. And the Lord said unto Moses, How long will this people provoke Me, and how long will it be ere they *believe Me?* As truly as I live, as ye have spoken in Mine ears, so will I do to you: your carcases SHALL fall in this widerness; and all that were numbered of you, according to your whole number, from twenty years old and upward, which have murmured against Me, doubtless ye shall not come into the land, concerning which I sware to make you dwell therein, *save Caleb the son of Jephunneh, and Joshua the son of Nun.* But your little ones, which ye said should be a prey, them will I bring in."

Happy Caleb! Happy Joshua! As it was to your father Abraham, so shall it be to you: your faith shall be counted to you for righteousness; and let who will perish, you shall be saved. "A thousand shall fall at thy side, and ten thousand at thy right hand; but it shall not come nigh thee. Only with thine eyes shalt thou behold and see the reward of the wicked. Because thou hast made the Lord thy habitation; there shall no evil befall thee, neither shall any plague come nigh thy dwelling." (Ps. xci. 7—10.)

Reader, God bless you. My last words to you are, that if we attempt it in reliance on God's Word, there is no single thing that He has commanded us to do, that we cannot do. Remember Caleb. Remember Joshua. Remember too the six hundred thousand who fell in the wilderness, because WITH GOD ON THEIR SIDE, they said, *We cannot.* Let a man live and die, saying, *I cannot,* and he is lost for ever.

XVIII.

The Conclusion.

YOU CANNOT. Nothing can be more true. In your own strength and power you can no more give up sin, turn to God, believe in Jesus Christ, and get through Him sanctification of the Spirit unto obedience, than these Israelites, of whom you have been reading, could have gone up unaided against the inhabitants of Canaan, and taken possession of their land. *You cannot :* but it is *because you cannot*, that God has given you a Saviour, to do for you and in you what it is so true you *cannot* do for yourself.

The Lord Jesus Christ, and Satan (for Satan can speak the truth if it suits him) both teach this truth : *you cannot.* A man, by the grace of God, has anxious moments about eternity, and feels a desire to be a Christian. The very first suggestion of the devil to such an one is, "There are circumstances in your case that make the thing impossible: YOU CANNOT." Now, so far he tells the truth; and the Lord Jesus Christ said exactly the same thing to His disciples, when He said, "Without Me, you can do nothing." But it is this "WITHOUT ME" that makes all the difference; and it is because we can do nothing to save ourselves that God has given us Jesus Christ. The very sinner who can do nothing, and who knows nothing until he knows and says, *I can do nothing*," is commanded to believe, on the warrant of God's Word, that *he can do all things through Christ, who strengtheneth him.* (Phil. iv. 13.)

The real ruin of the Israelites was that they forgot God their Saviour, and made their calculations *without Him.* They *forgot God* when they said and believed that they could not get into the promised land; and that man forgets God who says and believes that HE CANNOT BE A CHRISTIAN. The faith of both is the faith of the unbeliever, and they who hold it must perish. Has not God promised to save you, if you will go to Him? Has He not promised to forgive you all your sins for Christ's sake? Has He not promised to sanctify you for Christ's sake? Has He not promised that He will make Christ unto you "Wisdom, and Righteousness, and Sanctification, and Redemp-

tion?" Has He not told you that if you believe
in the Lord Jesus Christ you shall be saved?
Has He not said that if you trust in Him,
He will never leave you, nor forsake you?
Has He not told you that it was because you
were lost—*for that very reason;* because you had
destroyed yourself, but could not save yourself,—that God was manifest in the flesh, in
order that He might die *in the stead of sinners*, and so in virtue of what He had done,
be able to save to the uttermost them that
come to God by Him? Has He not told you
all this, and much more to the same effect, in
His Word? YOU KNOW HE HAS. Then refuse
to believe it, and say there is no hope for you;
refuse to believe it, and to go up in the strength
of it, against every sin and every difficulty, and
you are guilty of the identical sin of which
these Israelites were guilty, and for which God
sware in His wrath that they should never
enter into His rest. Nothing else could have
destroyed them. *Nothing else can destroy you.*

Though a host should encamp against you
then, be not afraid. Remember Caleb! Remember Joshua! Above all, remember "the
Lord reigneth!" the great I AM, and Jesus
Christ whom He hath sent. Such a faith will
be tried, and conflict with friends, and conflict

with foes will follow. Professors will wish to stone you; and you must fight with the sons of Anak; *all of which those Israelites escaped whose carcases fell in the wilderness :*—but the Lord will fight on your side; and, like Caleb and Joshua, you shall possess the gate of your enemies; nay more, as Caleb and Joshua not only rejoiced on earth in the fulfilment of all God's promises, but are now rejoicing in heaven; so when your warfare is accomplished, when God has led you into the wilderness and suffered you to hunger, to prove what is in your heart,—whether you will believe His Word, or not; if your faith fail not, if you believe not appearances, but in the living God, as surely as the day arrived when Caleb and Joshua entered into the promised land, so surely shall the day arrive when you shall also enter in; when you shall say with Paul, "I have fought the fight, I have kept the faith, I have finished my course;" and shall sit down in the heavenly Canaan, with Caleb, and Joshua, and Moses, and the blessed company of true Israelites,—the Church of God, which He has purchased with His own blood.

And now, reader, "the LORD bless thee, and keep thee: the LORD make His face shine upon thee, and be gracious unto thee. The

LORD lift up His countenance upon thee, and give thee peace." The children of Israel were about to go on a warfare when Moses took leave of them; and in His parting words I now take leave of you: "Be strong and of a good courage; fear not, nor be afraid; for the Lord thy God, He it is that doth go with thee; He will not fail thee, nor forsake thee."

Pray for me and for a blessing on this little book. Let him that thinketh he standeth take heed lest he fall. The history of these children of Israel has been recorded for our learning, and is "OURSELVES: A PICTURE.